MW01030071

A Journey
with Mark

The 50 Day Bible Challenge

This collection © 2015 Marek P. Zabriskie

Individual essays are the property of the authors.

All rights reserved.

ISBN: 978-0-88028-389-2

Printed in USA

Forward Movement
412 Sycamore Street
Cincinnati, OH 45202-4195
www.forwardmovement.org

A Journey with Mark

The 50 Day Bible Challenge

Edited by Marek P. Zabriskie

FORWARD MOVEMENT

Cincinnati, Ohio

Preface

The Bible Challenge began as a simple idea: to encourage daily reading of scripture. Simple ideas can bring forth great change.

Developing a daily spiritual discipline or practice is crucial for all Christians who wish to be faithful followers of Jesus. Saint Augustine and many other great Christians have written about the power of reading the Bible quietly on our own. There is no other book in the world that can so transform the human heart, motivate the human spirit, and give us the mind that was in Christ Jesus himself.

The Bible remains the world's best-selling book year after year. However, Episcopalians, Roman Catholics, and other mainline Christians often do not read it. Church historian and author Diana Butler Bass reports that among the 22,000 Christian groups and denominations in the United States, Episcopalians are the best-educated group but drop to nearly last when it comes to biblical literacy.

The goal of The Bible Challenge is to help individuals develop a lifelong, daily spiritual discipline of reading the Bible so that their lives may be constantly transformed and renewed. Studies reveal that prayerfully engaging scripture is the best way for Christians to grow in their faith and love of Jesus.

More than 250,000 persons in 2,500 churches in over forty countries are now participating in The Bible Challenge. We continue our partnership with Forward Movement with this new series—a focus on reading one book of the Bible over a fifty-day period. This book joins *A Journey with Matthew* and is the second in the series. This Bible Challenge series is an ideal resource for individuals, churches and dioceses during the Easter season or any time of the year.

Regular engagement with the Bible develops a strong Christian faith, enhances our experience of worship, and helps to create a more committed, articulate and contagious Christian. This is exactly what the world needs today.

With prayers and blessings for your faithful Bible reading,

The Rev. Marek P. Zabriskie
Founder of The Bible Challenge
Director of the Center for Biblical Studies
www.thecenterforbiblicalstudies.org
Rector of St. Thomas' Episcopal Church
Fort Washington, Pennsylvania

How to Read the Bible Prayerfully

Welcome to The 50 Day Bible Challenge. We are delighted that you are interested in reading God's life-transforming Word from the Gospel of Mark. It will change and enrich your life. Here are some suggestions to consider as you get started:

- You can begin The 50 Day Bible Challenge at any time of the year that you desire. It works especially well for the fifty days of Eastertide, beginning on Easter Day. It also could be read during Lent, beginning on the Sunday before Ash Wednesday.

- Each day has a manageable amount of reading, a meditation, a question or two, and a prayer, written by a host of wonderful authors.

- We suggest that you try to read the Bible each day. It is a great spiritual discipline to establish.

- If, however, you need more than fifty days to read through the Gospel of Mark, we support you in moving at the pace that works best for you.

- Many Bible Challenge participants read the Bible using their iPad, iPhone, Kindle, or Nook, or listen to the Bible on CDs or on a mobile device using Audio.com, faithcomesthroughhearing.org, or Pandora radio. Find what works for you.

- Our website, www.forwardmovement.org, offers many resources for learning more about the Bible and engaging in scripture. In addition, you can find a list of resources at www.thecenterforbiblicalresources.org. The center also offers a Read the Bible in a Year program and a Read the New Testament, Psalms, and Proverbs in a Year reading plans as well.

- Because the Bible is not a newspaper, it is best to read it with a reverent spirit. We advocate a devotional approach to reading the Bible, rather than reading it as a purely intellectual or academic exercise.

- Before reading the Bible, take a moment of silence to put yourself in the presence of God. We then invite you to read this prayer written by Archbishop Thomas Cranmer.

  Blessed Lord, who has caused all holy scriptures to be written for our learning: Grant us to hear them, read, mark, learn, and inwardly digest them, that we may embrace and ever hold fast the blessed hope of everlasting life, which you have given us in our Savior Jesus Christ; who lives and reigns with you and the Holy Spirit, one God, for ever and ever. Amen.

- Consider using the ancient monastic practice of *lectio divina*. In this form of Bible reading, you read the text and then meditate on a portion of it— be it a verse or two or even a single word. Mull over the words and their meaning. Then offer a prayer to God based on what you have read and how it has made you feel or what it has caused you to ponder. Listen in silence for God to respond to your prayer.

- We encourage you to read in the morning, if possible, so that your prayerful reading may spiritually enliven the rest of your day. If you cannot read in the morning, read when you can later in the day. Try to carve out a regular time for your daily reading.

- One way to hold yourself accountable to reading God's Word is to form a group within your church or community. By participating in The 50 Day Bible Challenge together, you can support one another in your reading, discuss the Bible passages, ask questions, and share how God's Word is transforming your life.

- If you do not want to join a group, you may wish to invite a friend or family member or two to share The 50 Day Bible Challenge with you.

- Put a notice in your church newsletter that you are starting a group to participate in The 50 Day Bible Challenge. Invite others to join you and to gather regularly to discuss the readings, ask questions, and share how it is transforming your life. Visit the Center for Biblical Resources website to see more suggestions about how churches can participate in The Bible Challenge.

- If you form a Bible Challenge group, consider holding a gathering or meal to celebrate your spiritual accomplishment.

- Have fun and find spiritual peace and the joy that God desires for you in your daily reading. The goal of the Center for Biblical Studies is to help you discover God's wisdom and to create a lifelong spiritual practice of daily Bible reading so that God may guide you through each day of your life.

- If you find reading the entire Bible and being part of The Bible Challenge to be a blessing in your life, then we strongly encourage you to share the blessing. Invite several friends or family members to participate in The Bible Challenge.

- Once you've finished one complete reading of the Bible, start over and do it again. God may speak differently to you in each reading. Follow the example of U.S. President John Adams, who read through the Bible each year during his adult life. We highly advocate this practice.

- After participating in The 50 Day Bible Challenge, you will be more able to support and mentor others in reading the Bible.

We are thrilled that you are participating in The Bible Challenge. May God richly bless you as you prayerfully engage the scriptures each day.

An Introduction to the Gospel of Mark

Mark is the shortest of the four gospels, only sixteen chapters long. It is tightly written, and the reader can move through it quickly. Yet, Mark is complex and nuanced. We can read and reread the text, constantly finding new things in it.

Most scholars believe that Mark was the first gospel set in writing. They also maintain that the authors of the gospels of Matthew and Luke had access to Mark and borrowed large amounts of it in writing their own accounts. Matthew and Luke also followed a similar chronology to the one developed by Mark. These three are known as the Synoptic Gospels, which in Greek means "capable of being seen together." The Gospel of John follows a different timeline and cannot be similarly examined side by side with the other gospels.

The gospels are not true biographies as we have come to understand biographies today. They do not present balanced accounts of Jesus' life. Nothing is told in the Gospel of Mark about Jesus' childhood or youth. He comes on the scene when he is around the age of thirty. And one quarter of this gospel focuses on the final week of Jesus' life.

Instead of telling Jesus' whole life story, this gospel has been carefully shaped from a theological perspective. It tells the story of God working through Jesus, God's only Son, to reconcile the world to himself, and to draw humanity closer to God. It is meant to form us spiritually, to remind us that we were created in God's image, placed on this planet for a purpose, and called to use our time, talents, and treasure to serve God faithfully.

As the first recorded account of Jesus' life, Mark's Gospel has often been the focal point for the quest for the historical Jesus and has been considered by many to be the most reliable historical source for understanding the life of Jesus. Despite its brevity, Mark is very sophisticated and uses compositional techniques that resemble the intricacies of some modern writers.

We do not know for certain who authored Mark's Gospel. Nor are we sure where or when it was written. Much speculation exists regarding all these questions. However it is generally believed that Mark concluded his work before the Roman War (67-70 CE). The intended audience is unknown, but we do know that they read Greek. Mark's mastery of the language, however, was far less sophisticated than that of other gospel writers, especially the author of Luke-Acts.

Mark did groundbreaking work, as he connected Jesus' life, ministry, and passion together into a coherent story. The gospel not only tells a story but also weaves a pattern of how God worked through Jesus. Jesus is given a variety of titles, including Christ, Teacher, Lord, Son of God, and Son of Man. In doing so, Mark presents Jesus in a way that a Greek-speaking audience could understand while also employing the language of the Torah to connect the story of Jesus with the Hebrew scripture.

Jesus' disciples are not always favorably represented by Mark. At times, they appear to be a hapless group who listen but do not understand and follow but do not know where they are going. Matthew and Luke later polish their image, portraying them as brighter and more capable of becoming the leaders of the early Church.

Mark frequently joins clauses with "and" or *kai* in Greek. The gospel also often employs the adverb "immediately" or *euthus* in Greek, which gives the narrative a sometimes frantic pace and a sense of rushing from one episode to another in Jesus' life.

There has been much controversy regarding the ending of the Gospel of Mark. The oldest and best manuscripts end at Mark 16:8, when the women arrive at the empty tomb to anoint Jesus' body. This shorter ending is a cliff-hanger, and we are left with a great mystery. Other manuscripts include the longer ending found in Mark 16:9-20. Still others insert a coda after Mark 16:8 as a bridge to 16:9-20. Textual criticism favors the shorter text. Based on this, it is believed that later scribes, who had access to Matthew's and Luke's gospels, added the longer ending.

This does not mean that Mark doubted the Resurrection of Christ. The message was that Jesus was not to be found among the dead. Jesus would be seen again, for he had arisen. The mysterious ending draws us back to the question at the center of Mark's Gospel: "Who do people say that I am?" Jesus asked this of his disciples in chapter 8 and he asks us the same question today. It is a question that no Christian or seeker can sidestep or avoid. We must each answer it for ourselves, and the answer that we give makes all the difference in how we lead our lives.

The Rev. Marek P. Zabriskie

A Journey
with Mark

The 50 Day Bible Challenge

Mark 1:1-11

1 The beginning of the good news of Jesus Christ, the Son of God.

²As it is written in the prophet Isaiah, "See, I am sending my messenger ahead of you, who will prepare your way; ³the voice of one crying out in the wilderness: 'Prepare the way of the Lord, make his paths straight,'"

⁴John the baptizer appeared in the wilderness, proclaiming a baptism of repentance for the forgiveness of sins. ⁵And people from the whole Judean countryside and all the people of Jerusalem were going out to him, and were baptized by him in the river Jordan, confessing their sins. ⁶Now John was clothed with camel's hair, with a leather belt around his waist, and he ate locusts and wild honey. ⁷He proclaimed, "The one who is more powerful than I is coming after me; I am not worthy to stoop down and untie the thong of his sandals. ⁸I have baptized you with water; but he will baptize you with the Holy Spirit."

⁹In those days Jesus came from Nazareth of Galilee and was baptized by John in the Jordan. ¹⁰And just as he was coming up out of the water, he saw the heavens torn apart and the Spirit descending like a dove on him. ¹¹And a voice came from heaven, "You are my Son, the Beloved; with you I am well pleased."

Reflection

Mark opens his account of the gospel with the story of Jesus' baptism. At the edge of the river Jordan, John was preaching a baptism of repentance, to prepare the people for the coming of the Messiah. In the midst of so many others seeking this baptism, Jesus comes without any announcement. He simply stands in line with everyone else. Unlike the other evangelists, Mark does not record the tussle between John and Jesus as to why Jesus insists on wading into the water. Mark simply says, "He was baptized by John."

The feast of the Baptism of our Lord is one of several principal days the Church designates for the celebration of baptism. Along with those who are born again by water and the Spirit, signed with the cross, and marked as Christ's own forever, we all renew the vows of our own baptism. We are reminded that, as missiologist Christopher Duraisingh puts it, "...baptism is primarily an event, as it was with the baptism of Christ, 'a solidarity plunge' in the waters of Jordan that flow through our neighborhoods today; that is, a commitment to walk in solidarity and compassion with others, sharing their hopes, tears, joy and pain. As such, baptism is fundamentally a missional act, an act of stepping out with Christ for a life for others." *

Our baptism immerses us in the affairs of our neighborhood, our nation, and the world. It marks us for ministry in the name of Christ's love, with justice and peace for all.

* "Church-Shaped Mission to Mission-Shaped Church," *Anglican Theological Review,* Winter 2010.

The Rt. Rev. Fred Hiltz
Primate of the Anglican Church of Canada
Toronto, Ontario

Questions

Of all the baptisms you have witnessed in your lifetime, do any stand out as absolutely soul moving? What made them so?

The one in the Jordon river!

For what special ministry are you marked through your vows of baptism? *I'm not sure I have a "special ministry"! I'm still doing a "walk in to righteousness" I hope — trusting in the leading of the Holy Spirit within! I guess my gift is I love people most of the time.*

Prayer

Eternal Father, who at the baptism of Jesus revealed him to be your Son, anointing him with the Holy Spirit, keep your children, born of water and the Spirit, faithful to their calling; through Jesus Christ our Lord, who lives and reigns with you and the Holy Spirit, one God, now and forever. *Amen.*

— *The Book of Alternative Services,*
The Anglican Church of Canada

Mark 1:12-20

[12]And the Spirit immediately drove him out into the wilderness. [13]He was in the wilderness forty days, tempted by Satan; and he was with the wild beasts; and the angels waited on him.

[14]Now after John was arrested, Jesus came to Galilee, proclaiming the good news of God, [15]and saying, "The time is fulfilled, and the kingdom of God has come near; repent, and believe in the good news." [16]As Jesus passed along the Sea of Galilee, he saw Simon and his brother Andrew casting a net into the sea—for they were fishermen. [17]And Jesus said to them, "Follow me and I will make you fish for people." [18]And immediately they left their nets and followed him. [19]As he went a little farther, he saw James son of Zebedee and his brother John, who were in their boat mending the nets. [20]Immediately he called them; and they left their father Zebedee in the boat with the hired men, and followed him.

Reflection

Today's reading carries us off into the wilderness. Without any extra narrative, Mark says that Jesus was driven out into the wilderness, tempted by Satan, and waited on by angels.

Then we are at the Sea of Galilee, where Jesus is announcing the coming of God's kingdom. Within a few days he is calling Andrew, Simon, James, and John to follow him in his mission. This little band will grow to include men and women, young and old, rich and poor. Jesus will form them into a community shaped through time by a pattern of being called and sent. This is the community we know as the Church, whose work it is to share good news, make disciples, help those in need, build a just world, and care for the earth. These are the Marks of Mission held by Anglicans worldwide.

Commenting on the second mark of mission, "to teach, baptize and nurture new believers," Edinburgh scholar Andrew Thompson says he is not comfortable with the distinction of "new" believers. It feels like there is "another class of established and settled ones, no longer in need of the nurture and teaching mandated for new believers."* He opts for an interpretation of "new" grounded in the image of the "new self" from the letter to the Colossians where Paul writes of stripping ourselves of the old self with its practices and clothing ourselves in Christ (3:9-10). This is the lifelong task of conversion to a manner of life in keeping with our vocation as those called and sent by Christ.

* *Life-Widening Mission: Global Anglican Perspectives,* 2012, Regnum Books International, p. 35.

The Rt. Rev. Fred Hiltz
Primate of the Anglican Church of Canada
Toronto, Ontario

A Journey with Mark

Question

In the point Andrew Thompson makes, there is a humility I find compelling and worthy of my own reflection. How does it strike you? Yes - humility is so important in my walk - I'm not sure how to grow in h because pride is so strong in me - I'm asking God to make me more aware when pride pops up!

Prayer

Draw your church together, O Lord, into one great company of disciples, together following our Lord Jesus Christ into every walk of life, together serving him in his mission to the world, and together witnessing to his love on every continent and island. We ask this in his name and for his sake. *Amen.*

— *The Book of Alternative Services,*
The Anglican Church of Canada

Lord, thank you for this book - may it help me to grow in humility realizing I am to be a servant as christ was. In his name I pray. Amen

Mark 1:21-45

[21]They went to Capernaum; and when the sabbath came, he entered the synagogue and taught. [22]They were astounded at his teaching, for he taught them as one having authority, and not as the scribes. [23]Just then there was in their synagogue a man with an unclean spirit, [24]and he cried out, "What have you to do with us, Jesus of Nazareth? Have you come to destroy us? I know who you are, the Holy One of God." [25]But Jesus rebuked him, saying, "Be silent, and come out of him!" [26]And the unclean spirit, convulsing him and crying with a loud voice, came out of him. [27]They were all amazed, and they kept on asking one another, "What is this? A new teaching—with authority! He commands even the unclean spirits, and they obey him." [28]At once his fame began to spread throughout the surrounding region of Galilee.

[29]As soon as they left the synagogue, they entered the house of Simon and Andrew, with James and John. [30]Now Simon's mother-in-law was in bed with a fever, and they told him about her at once. [31]He came and took her by the hand and lifted her up. Then the fever left her, and she began to serve them.

[32]That evening, at sundown, they brought to him all who were sick or possessed with demons. [33]And the whole city was gathered around the door. [34]And he cured many who were sick with various diseases, and cast out many demons; and he would not permit the demons to speak, because they knew him. [35]In the morning, while it was still very dark, he got up and went out to a deserted place,

and there he prayed. ³⁶And Simon and his companions hunted for him. ³⁷When they found him, they said to him, "Everyone is searching for you." ³⁸He answered, "Let us go on to the neighboring towns, so that I may proclaim the message there also; for that is what I came out to do." ³⁹And he went throughout Galilee, proclaiming the message in their synagogues and casting out demons.

⁴⁰A leper came to him begging him, and kneeling he said to him, "If you choose, you can make me clean." ⁴¹Moved with pity, Jesus stretched out his hand and touched him, and said to him, "I do choose. Be made clean!" ⁴²Immediately the leprosy left him, and he was made clean. ⁴³After sternly warning him he sent him away at once, ⁴⁴saying to him, "See that you say nothing to anyone; but go, show yourself to the priest, and offer for your cleansing what Moses commanded, as a testimony to them." ⁴⁵But he went out and began to proclaim it freely, and to spread the word, so that Jesus could no longer go into a town openly, but stayed out in the country; and people came to him from every quarter.

Reflection

The man in the synagogue is healed and unbound from his narrow religion and his rejection of Jesus' preaching. The people's response affirms Jesus as preacher and teacher of a new movement. Jesus is reforming the old religious ways. He challenges all Christians and Christian communities today, just as he challenged the faithful of his own day.

As Christians, we can be imprisoned by our religion, and Jesus seeks to free us from it. Jesus offers us unbounded love, free from the shackles of an inherited religion that says that you are not good enough to belong because you haven't earned God's love.

We as a community must be freed and unbound from the ties that bind us. You and I both know our own hearts. We know how hard it is to welcome others freely.

Jesus invites us to reach that part of our heart that believes in God's unfailing love. He invites us to be welcoming and accepting of others with abandon. We are invited to live lives in communities where the Holy One of God is present and alive and proclaimed. Most of all we are invited to proclaim with our lives the unbounded love of Jesus. We are invited to unbind one another from our self-made religious shackles and follow Jesus.

The Rt. Rev. Andrew Doyle
Bishop of the Diocese of Texas
Houston, Texas

Questions

In what ways has our practice of religion become more important than the message?

Is the benefit of Christian community lost when it becomes too difficult to belong?

What reforms are needed to bring our mission in line with a gospel of abundant grace?

"Decision" mag Billy Graham's article P.20 Jul/aug 2015 issue "Challenge for a Floundering Church" he lists 7 changes to save our churches!

Prayer

Heavenly Father, you have given us the gift of the Church and we have carved it into an idol of our hearts. Help us to see that our idea of church is in need of healing. Give us grace to seek to be a community of the kingdom of God where all find freedom. Cast out of our hearts the tired old religion of earned belonging, and help us to become communities of unbounded grace. *Amen.*

Mark 2:1-12

2 When he returned to Capernaum after some days, it was reported that he was at home. ²So many gathered around that there was no longer room for them, not even in front of the door; and he was speaking the word to them. ³Then some people came, bringing to him a paralyzed man, carried by four of them. ⁴And when they could not bring him to Jesus because of the crowd, they removed the roof above him; and after having dug through it, they let down the mat on which the paralytic lay. ⁵When Jesus saw their faith, he said to the paralytic, "Son, your sins are forgiven." ⁶Now some of the scribes were sitting there, questioning in their hearts, ⁷"Why does this fellow speak in this way? It is blasphemy! Who can forgive sins but God alone?" ⁸At once Jesus perceived in his spirit that they were discussing these questions among themselves; and he said to them, "Why do you raise such questions in your hearts? ⁹Which is easier, to say to the paralytic, 'Your sins are forgiven,' or to say, 'Stand up and take your mat and walk'? ¹⁰But so that you may know that the Son of Man has authority on earth to forgive sins" —he said to the paralytic— ¹¹"I say to you, stand up, take your mat and go to your home." ¹²And he stood up, and immediately took the mat and went out before all of them; so that they were all amazed and glorified God, saying, "We have never seen anything like this!"

Reflection

The religion of Jesus' day taught its followers that sin brought sickness and calamity upon the sinner. However, if the sinner repented, then the sin could be forgiven, the calamity averted, or the sickness healed. As in other passages, this story is not simply about a sick man and brave friends. It is about God's amazing power to do religion differently.

Jesus does not wait for the man to repent and ask for forgiveness. Jesus does not wait for the religion of his day to say that this man is healed or forgiven. Jesus does not make excuses about why he cannot respond because of the circumstances. Instead, Jesus heals the man and forgives his sins. Why? Because through his actions, Jesus reveals to us that God's love is unbounded, God's forgiveness is complete, and God's healing is an all-powerful balm.

We can get caught up in the gospel writer's vision of these devoted friends lowering the man through a hole in the roof so that Jesus might heal him. It's an extraordinary effort! Our religious hearts want us to find that the man or his friends earned Jesus' blessing. But it is not there. God's grace is not subject to an economic exchange. What the crowd in the gospel witnessed is proof of a loving, healing, and powerful God who gives away grace to people who may not deserve it. That is God's nature.

The Rt. Rev. Andrew Doyle
Bishop of The Diocese of Texas
Houston, Texas

Questions _____

Who are the people in your life that you feel have not earned your forgiveness? *none*

What relationships are still bound because you don't think they have done enough? God forgives them and forgives you. Can you forgive yourself? *am working on that*

What do you think keeps you from taking up your mat and walking? *I guess I still wonder if I deserve it - I'm not sure - my thumb hurts - hard to write!*

Prayer _____

Forgiving and healing God, in Jesus you showed us that all are forgiven, and that I am forgiven. Help me to see your grace at work in my life and to respond by forgiving myself. Then let me hear clearly your call to take up my life and do the same for others. Help me to be a sign of your redemption that is eager to forgive, ready to heal, and filled with love. *Amen.*

Mark 2:13-17

[13]Jesus went out again beside the sea; the whole crowd gathered around him, and he taught them. [14]As he was walking along, he saw Levi son of Alphaeus sitting at the tax booth, and he said to him, "Follow me." And he got up and followed him. [15]And as he sat at dinner in Levi's house, many tax collectors and sinners were also sitting with Jesus and his disciples—for there were many who followed him. [16]When the scribes of the Pharisees saw that he was eating with sinners and tax collectors, they said to his disciples, "Why does he eat with tax collectors and sinners?" [17]When Jesus heard this, he said to them, "Those who are well have no need of a physician, but those who are sick; I have come to call not the righteous but sinners."

Reflection

Levi is a strange name. There are in fact only four men in the whole of scripture who bear that name. But it is not the frequency of the name that matters. Rather it is its significance, the associations the name brings with it, the implied connections. The first Levi—and the one we know best—was the third son of Jacob and Leah. More to the point, he was the progenitor of the tribe of Levi, the line of sacred priests in Judaism. Here is Jesus, hundreds of years later, calling this man—this first-century Levi—to follow him, and Levi does.

Indeed Levi not only follows but also goes so far as to offer Jesus food and drink that our Lord sits down to openly enjoy in Levi's house. The only discordant note in their encounter is that the sociopolitical religious order of Pharisees and their scribes are not invited to participate but rebuffed and chastised. Our Lord tells them that he and Levi have business together. It is a holy and healthy business that those who consider themselves to be righteous and correct may never be able to enter into unless they can lay aside the illness of self-affirmation and culturally defined holiness.

Phyllis Tickle
Author and speaker
Millington, Tennessee

A Journey with Mark

Question

Jesus often spoke in aphorisms that we quote frequently, and often thoughtlessly—ones such as "only the sick have need of a physician." But what does it really mean to recognize one's self as standing in need of the Great Physician?

Pride has 2 shapes - 1 - good feeling of self - worth in my life & 2 - forgetting where that comes from - thinking its from me!

Prayer

Deliver me, dear Lord, from the crippling sin of self-affirmation, and make me, like Levi, both humble enough and grateful enough to receive you always and everywhere into myself. *Amen.*

Father, nudge me please when I forget - keep me in true humility.

Mark 2:18-28

18Now John's disciples and the Pharisees were fasting; and people came and said to him, "Why do John's disciples and the disciples of the Pharisees fast, but your disciples do not fast?" 19Jesus said to them, "The wedding guests cannot fast while the bridegroom is with them, can they? As long as they have the bridegroom with them, they cannot fast. 20The days will come when the bridegroom is taken away from them, and then they will fast on that day.

21"No one sews a piece of unshrunk cloth on an old cloak; otherwise, the patch pulls away from it, the new from the old, and a worse tear is made. 22And no one puts new wine into old wineskins; otherwise, the wine will burst the skins, and the wine is lost, and so are the skins; but one puts new wine into fresh wineskins."

23One sabbath he was going through the grainfields; and as they made their way his disciples began to pluck heads of grain. 24The Pharisees said to him, "Look, why are they doing what is not lawful on the sabbath?" 25And he said to them, "Have you never read what David did when he and his companions were hungry and in need of food? 26He entered the house of God, when Abiathar was high priest, and ate the bread of the Presence, which it is not lawful for any but the priests to eat, and he gave some to his companions." 27Then he said to them, "The sabbath was made for humankind, and not humankind for the sabbath; 28so the Son of Man is lord even of the sabbath."

Reflection

Our Lord famously spoke in the cryptic aphorisms typical of an ancient wisdom teacher. Nowhere is there a better example of his use of such proverbs and folk sayings than in this passage from Mark. One right after another, he fires them off at his critics and accusers. Do wedding guests fast at a wedding? Does anybody in his right mind patch an old garment with new, unshrunken material? Does any sane person put fermenting wine into previously used skins that have lost their elasticity?

Yet there is probably no section of Jesus' teachings that has more burning relevance for our own times. We live in change, indeed in an era of massive, almost unprecedented change. And the biggest part of this change cries out to us for prayer and thought about what being Church really means here and today.

Phyllis Tickle
Author and speaker
Millington, Tennessee

Questions

Can we dare to fashion new wineskins for our new wine? If so, how do we do it?

What indeed does it mean to make the Son of Man, and not the tradition of the elders, the substance of our worship?

Prayer

O Father of us and of all time, be merciful as we struggle to be Church even as Church is changing and shifting around us, and even as there seems to be no cohesion among us. Show us the way, Father, to understand Christ as Lord of the sabbath every day of our lives. *Amen.*

Mark 3:1-12

3 Again he entered the synagogue, and a man was there who had a withered hand. ²They watched him to see whether he would cure him on the sabbath, so that they might accuse him. ³And he said to the man who had the withered hand, "Come forward." ⁴Then he said to them, "Is it lawful to do good or to do harm on the sabbath, to save life or to kill?" But they were silent. ⁵He looked around at them with anger; he was grieved at their hardness of heart and said to the man, "Stretch out your hand." He stretched it out, and his hand was restored. ⁶The Pharisees went out and immediately conspired with the Herodians against him, how to destroy him. ⁷Jesus departed with his disciples to the sea, and a great multitude from Galilee followed him; ⁸hearing all that he was doing, they came to him in great numbers from Judea, Jerusalem, Idumea, beyond the Jordan, and the region around Tyre and Sidon. ⁹He told his disciples to have a boat ready for him because of the crowd, so that they would not crush him; ¹⁰for he had cured many, so that all who had diseases pressed upon him to touch him. ¹¹Whenever the unclean spirits saw him, they fell down before him and shouted, "You are the Son of God!" ¹²But he sternly ordered them not to make him known.

Reflection

There aren't many times when we read that Jesus gets mad. Perhaps the most notable example is described in all four of the gospels, as Jesus clears the temple of money changers, reacting to ways that the spirit of religion had been corrupted and its core message obscured. In this third chapter of Mark, Jesus' anger similarly surfaces in response to the religious leaders of his day. It's a story about Jesus' healing power, a central feature of his ministry, and a call to address the brokenness of the world wherever he saw it.

But this is more than a healing story. When given the opportunity to offer healing, Jesus goes for it, even if this flies in the face of traditional observance. One might have anticipated joy on the part of religious leaders, celebration of the possible healing of this broken man. But, locked in their prison of what ought to be, these leaders can't see past the rules to notice the miracle.

Jesus calls them to the way of compassion, the spirit of religion that has been obscured. He grieves over their hardness of heart. I wonder how he still grieves over our hardness of heart, our eyes closed to human need, our clinging to tradition at the expense of healing human contact, our fear of fresh expressions of God's love, and our failure to conduct our lives with compassion. Like the religious leaders of Jesus' time, we can miss the miracles in front of us.

The Rev. Jay Sidebotham
Director of RenewalWorks,
a ministry of Forward Movement
Wilmington, North Carolina

A Journey with Mark

Questions

Do the religious rules, traditions, and conventions you hold limit or support your ability to show compassion? Are there ways in which you are silent to the needs of the world around you?

Have you experienced hardness of heart? What have been ways that a hardened heart has changed?

Prayer

Deliver us, good Lord, from hardness of heart. Open our hearts to your grace and truth. May we be watchful for ways to be instruments of your healing power and compassion, even if that means moving beyond our comfort zones to places where your healing love can meet the needs of our broken world. We pray in the name of Christ, the healer. *Amen.*

Mark 3:13-19

¹³He went up the mountain and called to him those whom he wanted, and they came to him. ¹⁴And he appointed twelve, whom he also named apostles, to be with him, and to be sent out to proclaim the message, ¹⁵and to have authority to cast out demons. ¹⁶So he appointed the twelve: Simon (to whom he gave the name Peter); ¹⁷James son of Zebedee and John the brother of James (to whom he gave the name Boanerges, that is, Sons of Thunder); ¹⁸and Andrew, and Philip, and Bartholomew, and Matthew, and Thomas, and James son of Alphaeus, and Thaddaeus, and Simon the Cananaean, ¹⁹and Judas Iscariot, who betrayed him.

Then he went home.

Reflection

Jesus named apostles, also referred to as disciples. What's the difference? Disciples were followers, those who learned from Jesus, perhaps like a gaggle of medical students who follow a doctor around from room to room in a teaching hospital, learning as they go. They were apostles as well. We know a fair amount about some of them. Others are little more than names to us. But as apostles, they had this in common: Called by Jesus, they were sent out into the world to do God's work.

They also had something else in common: From what we know of them, they were hardly perfect people. Peter denied, James and John jockeyed for corner offices. Thomas doubted. Judas betrayed. When the cross was raised up, they all ran. Yet with all their flaws, they founded the church. They were sent into the world and turned it around. That is good news for each one of us.

As the eucharist reminds us, we are sent into the world to do God's work. What will that ministry look like today? It's been said that the dismissal may well be the most important part of our liturgy, as reflected in a sign I saw posted over the exit of one church's nave: "The worship is over. The service begins." As the Church, we carry on the work of these apostles, not because we are so special, but because we are called. What is God sending you into the world to do and be today?

The Rev. Jay Sidebotham
Director of RenewalWorks,
a ministry of Forward Movement
Wilmington, North Carolina

Questions

Today, how can you take a step as a disciple, a follower, or student of Jesus?

If you were asked to describe yourself as an apostle—someone sent into the world to do God's work—what would you say?

How can you be an apostle—someone sent into the world to proclaim by word and example the good news?

Prayer

Gracious God, you send us into the world to love and serve with gladness and singleness of heart. Give us strength to be both disciples and apostles. Help us always to learn and to follow. Give us a sense of your mission in the world. Help us to recall that as we go forward, your strength accompanies us on the way. *Amen.*

A Journey with Mark

Mark 3:20-35

20and the crowd came together again, so that they could not even eat. 21When his family heard it, they went out to restrain him, for people were saying, "He has gone out of his mind." 22And the scribes who came down from Jerusalem said, "He has Beelzebul, and by the ruler of the demons he casts out demons." 23And he called them to him, and spoke to them in parables, "How can Satan cast out Satan? 24If a kingdom is divided against itself, that kingdom cannot stand. 25And if a house is divided against itself, that house will not be able to stand. 26And if Satan has risen up against himself and is divided, he cannot stand, but his end has come. 27But no one can enter a strong man's house and plunder his property without first tying up the strong man; then indeed the house can be plundered.

28"Truly I tell you, people will be forgiven for their sins and whatever blasphemies they utter; 29but whoever blasphemes against the Holy Spirit can never have forgiveness, but is guilty of an eternal sin"— 30for they had said, "He has an unclean spirit."

31Then his mother and his brothers came; and standing outside, they sent to him and called him. 32A crowd was sitting around him; and they said to him, "Your mother and your brothers and sisters are outside, asking for you." 33And he replied, "Who are my mother and my brothers?" 34And looking at those who sat around him, he said, "Here are my mother and my brothers! 35Whoever does the will of God is my brother and sister and mother."

Reflection

This passage describes opposition that Jesus experiences from insiders and outsiders—his family and scribes from Jerusalem. Jesus' family says he's crazy, while some scribes say that he is possessed. This is a divided household. But who is the first group? The New Revised Standard translation of "family" is a conjecture. Both the King James Version and Tyndale's translations describe the same group differently: "friends" or "kinsmen" (KJV) and "they that longed unto him" (Tyndale). The Greek phrase is "his own" or "a group of his," which can mean family but can also indicate another group.

Where else does the phrase or something like it appear in this gospel? Mark 1:36 refers to Simon and his companions with a similar phrase, identifying Andrew, James, and John. So perhaps the story in verse 21 refers to a group of companions or disciples. In the surrounding context, "a group of his" or "his own" could refer to the twelve, who go with Jesus into a house and come out to restrain him forcibly very soon after being called by him.

Perhaps Mark is emphasizing that the disciples are selected by Jesus and then immediately attempt to restrain him in the same way that Judas is simultaneously appointed and identified as the one who betrayed him (3:19).

If this is the case, then Jesus' mother and brothers are not introduced until verse 31. This is the first time we see them, standing outside and calling to him. Jesus does nothing to move toward them. Responding to the observation of the crowd that they are standing outside, Jesus replies to those sitting around him, "Who are my mother and my brothers?" Here he identifies as family those who do the will of God rather than those who are actually his kin. The boundaries of this newly constituted familial group are permeable. Its membership includes brothers, sisters, and mothers, but not fathers. Only God is to be called Father.

Deirdre Good
Professor of New Testament,
The General Theological Seminary
New York, New York

Question _____

When have you, like Jesus, experienced opposition from friends or those around you? You may find Psalm 27:10 helpful: "If my father and mother forsake me, the Lord will take me up."

Prayer _____

O God, you are far beyond us yet as near as a parent. We thank you for our households and families: those from which we come and those we create. Put far from us intolerance, fear, and hatred. Strengthen amongst us the bonds of patience, kindness, and charity that we may be knit together into a community of love to your honor and glory. In Jesus' name we pray. *Amen.*

Mark 4:1-20

4 Again he began to teach beside the sea. Such a very large crowd gathered around him that he got into a boat on the sea and sat there, while the whole crowd was beside the sea on the land. [2]He began to teach them many things in parables, and in his teaching he said to them: [3]"Listen! A sower went out to sow. [4]And as he sowed, some seed fell on the path, and the birds came and ate it up. [5]Other seed fell on rocky ground, where it did not have much soil, and it sprang up quickly, since it had no depth of soil. [6]And when the sun rose, it was scorched; and since it had no root, it withered away. [7]Other seed fell among thorns, and the thorns grew up and choked it, and it yielded no grain. [8]Other seed fell into good soil and brought forth grain, growing up and increasing and yielding thirty and sixty and a hundredfold." [9]And he said, "Let anyone with ears to hear listen!"

[10]When he was alone, those who were around him along with the twelve asked him about the parables. [11]And he said to them, "To you has been given the secret of the kingdom of God, but for those outside, everything comes in parables; [12]in order that 'they may indeed look, but not perceive, and may indeed listen, but not understand; so that they may not turn again and be forgiven.'"

[13]And he said to them, "Do you not understand this parable? Then how will you understand all the parables? [14]The sower sows the word. [15]These are the ones on the path where the word is sown: when they hear, Satan immediately comes and takes away the word that is

sown in them. [16]And these are the ones sown on rocky ground: when they hear the word, they immediately receive it with joy. [17]But they have no root, and endure only for a while; then, when trouble or persecution arises on account of the word, immediately they fall away. [18]And others are those sown among the thorns: these are the ones who hear the word, [19]but the cares of the world, and the lure of wealth, and the desire for other things come in and choke the word, and it yields nothing. [20]And these are the ones sown on the good soil: they hear the word and accept it and bear fruit, thirty and sixty and a hundredfold."

Reflection

Jesus often spoke using parables. He didn't invent the genre, but as we see from Matthew, Mark, and Luke, parables were central to Jesus' message of God's realm. The first time Jesus speaks in Mark, he tells the parable of the sower. The parable does not describe an actual event but rather something beyond itself.

Mark's explanation of the parable follows the parable itself, saying that what is sown is the word, which is heard by those who are cynical, distracted, those who are half-hearted, and those who are true believers. Two thousand years of interpretation propose that the parable is about the sower or the best way to hear the word. But if the emphasis in the parable is on the sower, or the true believers, then why does the parable describe three other types of receptivity?

It's clear that the disciples could not understand Jesus' parables and had to have Jesus explain the parables to them (Mark 4:34). Compounding the problem is that Jesus explains everything in parables "in order that they may indeed look, but not perceive, and may indeed listen, but not understand." Jesus says in Mark (and in Matthew) that the function of parables is to prevent understanding. Parables in fact drive people away. They repel the distracted listener, the hard-hearted, the cynical, and the lukewarm.

Parables require listeners to work at understanding. Jesus uses parables such as the sower and the language of metaphor to invite hearers to train themselves to see the world from God's point of view.

Deirdre Good
Professor of New Testament,
The General Theological Seminary
New York, New York

Question

Why do you think Jesus teaches in parables according to Matthew, Mark, and Luke?

Prayer

Cultivate in us, O God, a love of your word. Open our ears to hear, our hearts to receive, and our minds to understand. Give us patience and tenacity as we seek to discern your presence here on earth. Give us courage to do your will. In Jesus' name we pray. *Amen.*

Mark 4:21-34

[21]He said to them, "Is a lamp brought in to be put under the bushel basket, or under the bed, and not on the lampstand? [22]For there is nothing hidden, except to be disclosed; nor is anything secret, except to come to light. [23]Let anyone with ears to hear listen!" [24]And he said to them, "Pay attention to what you hear; the measure you give will be the measure you get, and still more will be given you. [25]For to those who have, more will be given; and from those who have nothing, even what they have will be taken away."

[26]He also said, "The kingdom of God is as if someone would scatter seed on the ground, [27]and would sleep and rise night and day, and the seed would sprout and grow, he does not know how. [28]The earth produces of itself, first the stalk, then the head, then the full grain in the head. [29]But when the grain is ripe, at once he goes in with his sickle, because the harvest has come."

[30]He also said, "With what can we compare the kingdom of God, or what parable will we use for it? [31]It is like a mustard seed, which, when sown upon the ground, is the smallest of all the seeds on earth; [32]yet when it is sown it grows up and becomes the greatest of all shrubs, and puts forth large branches, so that the birds of the air can make nests in its shade."

[33]With many such parables he spoke the word to them, as they were able to hear it; [34]he did not speak to them except in parables, but he explained everything in private to his disciples.

Reflection

There's a power in stories that goes far beyond the power of facts, data, or statistics. Stories move us. Stories connect us to the information we are hearing in deeper, more intimate ways. Stories color our views and touch our feelings and our souls in ways that mere facts never can. We remember important moments in life through story. We remember important information because we or someone else has connected us through the story.

In this passage, we hear Jesus' teaching about the kingdom of God through story. "With many such parables [stories], he spoke the word to them...; he did not speak to them except in parables." Jesus understood what so many of us understand: There's a power in telling stories, even short, pithy ones that convey a deeper meaning. And Jesus was a master storyteller.

In the short stories of this passage from Mark, Jesus describes the kingdom of God at work in our lives and in the world. It is not overpowering or even obvious. It is a small light, a small piece of the truth, a sense of justice. It is the tiniest seed that is transformed into the tallest of shrubs, providing shelter and safety. Jesus wants us to understand that from a little, God's kingdom enters into our lives, and from our small offering, God can make an abundance.

The Rev. W. Frank Allen
Rector of St. David's (Radnor) Church
Wayne, Pennsylvania

A Journey with Mark

Question

Where might God be calling you to use some gift, small though it may be, to make God's kingdom known to others?

Today I stayed with Bert
for 2 hrs - I brought lunch. We
had a good time visiting.
She is so frail - God bless her.
Then I met Susan who came.

Prayer

Loving God, thank you for the gifts great and small that grace our lives. Help us to remember the stories of your great love for us and empower us to offer our gifts for your purposes and your coming kingdom. This we ask in Jesus' name. *Amen.*

Mark 4:35-41

[35]On that day, when evening had come, he said to them, "Let us go across to the other side." [36]And leaving the crowd behind, they took him with them in the boat, just as he was. Other boats were with him. [37]A great windstorm arose, and the waves beat into the boat, so that the boat was already being swamped. [38]But he was in the stern, asleep on the cushion; and they woke him up and said to him, "Teacher, do you not care that we are perishing?" [39]He woke up and rebuked the wind, and said to the sea, "Peace! Be still!" Then the wind ceased, and there was a dead calm. [40]He said to them, "Why are you afraid? Have you still no faith?" [41]And they were filled with great awe and said to one another, "Who then is this, that even the wind and the sea obey him?"

Reflection

The Sea of Galilee is most often a calm, placid body of water with homes and towns built right up to the edge of the water. On most days, fishermen and tourists still ply the waters during the day and through the night. But when the temperature shifts and the wind blows from the west, warmer air funnels through the surrounding hills. The waves roil, and six- to eight-foot seas turn the lake from peaceful to a turbulent intensity that can be life threatening. And in this kind of storm, Jesus speaks, "Peace!" and rebukes the storm, bringing back the calm.

Our lives are often filled with peaceful or at least mundane days, until, inevitably, the storms come. A tree falls on our car in the driveway. A relationship of many years bends to almost breaking. We or someone we love is struck by a life-threatening illness. The peace of our lives is taken away in an instant.

Here too, Jesus speaks a word of peace, rebuking the storms in our lives with his presence, power, and grace, changing us and the circumstance we face.

The Rev. W. Frank Allen
Rector of St. David's (Radnor) Church
Wayne, Pennsylvania.

Questions

When in your life or the life of someone you know have you sensed the power of Christ calming the storm? How so?

Prayer

O Lord, our times are in your hands. Open our hearts and lives to your presence. Calm the storms of our lives that we may know your love and mercy and live each day in hope for whatever comes our way. In Jesus' name we pray. *Amen.*

Mark 5:1-20

5 They came to the other side of the sea, to the country of the Gerasenes. ²And when he had stepped out of the boat, immediately a man out of the tombs with an unclean spirit met him. ³He lived among the tombs; and no one could restrain him any more, even with a chain; ⁴for he had often been restrained with shackles and chains, but the chains he wrenched apart, and the shackles he broke in pieces; and no one had the strength to subdue him. ⁵Night and day among the tombs and on the mountains he was always howling and bruising himself with stones. ⁶When he saw Jesus from a distance, he ran and bowed down before him; ⁷and he shouted at the top of his voice, "What have you to do with me, Jesus, Son of the Most High God? I adjure you by God,

do not torment me." ⁸For he had said to him, "Come out of the man, you unclean spirit!" ⁹Then Jesus asked him, "What is your name?" He replied, "My name is Legion; for we are many." ¹⁰He begged him earnestly not to send them out of the country. ¹¹Now there on the hillside a great herd of swine was feeding; ¹²and the unclean spirits begged him, "Send us into the swine; let us enter them." ¹³So he gave them permission. And the unclean spirits came out and entered the swine; and the herd, numbering about two thousand, rushed down the steep bank into the sea, and were drowned in the sea.

¹⁴The swineherds ran off and told it in the city and in the country. Then people came to see what it was that had happened. ¹⁵They came to Jesus

and saw the demoniac sitting there, clothed and in his right mind, the very man who had had the legion; and they were afraid. [16]Those who had seen what had happened to the demoniac and to the swine reported it. [17]Then they began to beg Jesus to leave their neighborhood. [18]As he was getting into the boat, the man who had been possessed by demons begged him that he might be with him. [19]But Jesus refused, and said to him, "Go home to your friends, and tell them how much the Lord has done for you, and what mercy he has shown you." [20]And he went away and began to proclaim in the Decapolis how much Jesus had done for him; and everyone was amazed.

Reflection

Demons and swine. This is not the stuff of our daily lives, yet this story is not as foreign to us as we might wish. The baptismal service in *The Book of Common Prayer* asks candidates for baptism—or the sponsors of those too young to answer for themselves: "Do you renounce the sinful desires that draw you from the love of God?" The reply comes quickly: "I renounce them." Easier said than done though. We all know what our failings are, our besetting sins, even if we prefer not to call them by that name. We know too just how persistent they are. The chains and shackles we devise and our attempts to control them too often give way, leaving us bruised, anguished, and isolated.

Jesus crossed the Sea of Galilee intending to begin a mission of healing and teaching; he leaves having healed only this one man. The townspeople, the man's neighbors, want Jesus gone. Jesus' work of healing disrupts the local economy (all those pigs) and disturbs the peace they have made with the sin and pain in their midst. Yet new life for this one man was clearly worth the journey. Jesus expresses no regret and tells the man, now restored and in his right mind, to proclaim what the Lord has done for him. The life of this man will be a powerful lesson to all he meets about the grace and mercy of God. Jesus' teaching continues whenever we proclaim the new life we have received through his grace and healing.

The Rev. Brenda G. Husson
Rector of St. James' Church Fifth Avenue
New York, New York

Questions

As you reflect on your own life, where do you feel battered and bruised?

Can you believe that, for Jesus, you are always worth the journey?

Who do you know who might need to hear your story of Jesus' healing love?

Prayer

Gracious and loving Lord, you come to us even when we believe it is too late or we are too broken. Thank you for making the journey to us and for your commitment to restore us in body, mind, and spirit. Teach us to look for your coming and to share with others the gifts we have received from your overflowing grace. *Amen.*

Mark 5:21-43

²¹When Jesus had crossed again in the boat to the other side, a great crowd gathered around him; and he was by the sea. ²²Then one of the leaders of the synagogue named Jairus came and, when he saw him, fell at his feet ²³and begged him repeatedly, "My little daughter is at the point of death. Come and lay your hands on her, so that she may be made well, and live."

²⁴So he went with him. And a large crowd followed him and pressed in on him. ²⁵Now there was a woman who had been suffering from hemorrhages for twelve years. ²⁶She had endured much under many physicians, and had spent all that she had; and she was no better, but rather grew worse. ²⁷She had heard about Jesus, and came up behind him in the crowd and touched his cloak, ²⁸for she said, "If I but touch his clothes, I will be made well." ²⁹Immediately her hemorrhage stopped; and she felt in her body that she was healed of her disease. ³⁰Immediately aware that power had gone forth from him, Jesus turned about in the crowd and said, "Who touched my clothes?" ³¹And his disciples said to him, "You see the crowd pressing in on you; how can you say, 'Who touched me?'" ³²He looked all around to see who had done it. ³³But the woman, knowing what had happened to her, came in fear and trembling, fell down before him, and told him the whole truth. ³⁴He said to her, "Daughter, your faith has made you well; go in peace, and be healed of your disease."

³⁵While he was still speaking, some people came from the

leader's house to say, "Your daughter is dead. Why trouble the teacher any further?" [36]But overhearing what they said, Jesus said to the leader of the synagogue, "Do not fear, only believe." [37]He allowed no one to follow him except Peter, James, and John, the brother of James. [38]When they came to the house of the leader of the synagogue, he saw a commotion, people weeping and wailing loudly. [39]When he had entered, he said to them, "Why do you make a commotion and weep? The child is not dead but sleeping."

[40]And they laughed at him. Then he put them all outside, and took the child's father and mother and those who were with him, and went in where the child was. [41]He took her by the hand and said to her, "Talitha cum," which means, "Little girl, get up!" [42]And immediately the girl got up and began to walk about (she was twelve years of age). At this they were overcome with amazement. [43]He strictly ordered them that no one should know this, and told them to give her something to eat.

Reflection

Desperate times call for desperate measures. A child sick unto death, a debilitating disorder. Both Jairus and the woman with a years-long hemorrhage know about desperation. Both behave inappropriately. For a leader of the synagogue to fall at the feet of an itinerant preacher and beg for help exposes the limits of his knowledge and authority. He does not care. He simply hopes Jesus will heal his daughter. The constant flow of blood has left this woman perpetually exhausted; it has made her ritually unclean as well. For a woman to reach out and touch a man not closely related to her is unacceptable, not to mention defiling. She does not care. She simply hopes proximity to Jesus will heal her. Inappropriate behavior does not concern Jesus. In their desperate acts he sees faith.

"Your faith has made you well." Sometimes we hear Jesus' words and they become a source of pain for us: "If I only had more faith, then God would have healed me." Sometimes Christians say to others, "If you only have faith, Jesus will heal you" and then if healing does not come, guilt is added to the burden of a person already weighed down and distressed. What Jesus commends is the longing for healing and renewal that makes us seek him out. It may be born of desperation, but if it helps us push through the clutter, the crowds, or the naysayers to reach him, then that is faith enough. How and when healing comes is up to God. In our asking, we declare our faith in God's promise of new life.

The Rev. Brenda G. Husson
Rector of St. James' Church Fifth Avenue
New York, New York

Questions

Have there been times when your own need to behave appropriately has kept you from reaching out to Jesus or telling him what you need?

Can you take some time in prayer to tell Jesus where you long for healing and renewal?

Prayer

Dear Lord, sometimes I'm afraid that I don't have enough faith. Help me to remember that my desire for you is faith enough, then kindle that desire within me that I might daily call upon your name and look to you for my life and my salvation. *Amen.*

Mark 6:1-13

6 He left that place and came to his hometown, and his disciples followed him. ²On the sabbath he began to teach in the synagogue, and many who heard him were astounded. They said, "Where did this man get all this? What is this wisdom that has been given to him? What deeds of power are being done by his hands! ³Is not this the carpenter, the son of Mary and brother of James and Joses and Judas and Simon, and are not his sisters here with us?" And they took offense at him. ⁴Then Jesus said to them, "Prophets are not without honor, except in their hometown, and among their own kin, and in their own house." ⁵And he could do no deed of power there, except that he laid his hands on a few sick people and cured them. ⁶And he was amazed at their unbelief.

Then he went about among the villages teaching. ⁷He called the twelve and began to send them out two by two, and gave them authority over the unclean spirits. ⁸He ordered them to take nothing for their journey except a staff; no bread, no bag, no money in their belts; ⁹but to wear sandals and not to put on two tunics. ¹⁰He said to them, "Wherever you enter a house, stay there until you leave the place. ¹¹If any place will not welcome you and they refuse to hear you, as you leave, shake off the dust that is on your feet as a testimony against them." ¹²So they went out and proclaimed that all should repent. ¹³They cast out many demons, and anointed with oil many who were sick and cured them.

Reflection

In the well-known and often re-shown movie, *The Blues Brothers*, there is one consistent cure for whatever seemed to be troubling main characters Jake and Elwood: a road trip. In this passage, Jesus' leadership with the disciples gives evidence that the Blues Brothers did not invent this bit of therapeutic intervention.

When Jesus was rejected by his own hometown—perhaps an experience many of us have had at one time or another—he had to make some choices. Jesus could have moped around and wallowed in self-pity. We all know what this looks like, and we know that such people are hard to be around, even for a short period of time. However, Jesus was a spiritual leader who had a responsibility to his Father and to his followers. As a spiritual leader he knew there was another and more positive path of action. Though somewhat astonished at his rejection, Jesus chose action over inaction. He directed his followers to get going on a road trip with instructions to spread God's message of healing care and redemptive love to everyone who would listen—all those who had ears to hear.

When you are shunned, rejected, or even humiliated, it is inevitable that you will react. Your selection of a reaction will be a strong indicator of who you follow and to whom you belong. Choose wisely and prayerfully.

The Rt. Rev. James B. Magness
Bishop Suffragan for the
Armed Forces and Federal Ministries
Washington, DC

Questions

Looking back on your life, how have you responded to personal rejection and mistreatment?

Against the field of all possible responses, how might you have chosen a more constructive and prayerful action?

Prayer

Holy and life-giving God, at times it seems to be outside of our spiritual makeup to respond positively when others hurt us. Help us to change so that daily we might grow more into the likeness of your Son, our Lord Jesus, in whose name we pray. *Amen.*

Mark 6:14-29

[14]King Herod heard of it, for Jesus' name had become known. Some were saying, "John the baptizer has been raised from the dead; and for this reason these powers are at work in him." [15]But others said, "It is Elijah." And others said, "It is a prophet, like one of the prophets of old." [16]But when Herod heard of it, he said, "John, whom I beheaded, has been raised."

[17]For Herod himself had sent men who arrested John, bound him, and put him in prison on account of Herodias, his brother Philip's wife, because Herod had married her. [18]For John had been telling Herod, "It is not lawful for you to have your brother's wife." [19]And Herodias had a grudge against him, and wanted to kill him. But she could not, [20]for Herod feared John, knowing that he was a righteous and holy man, and he protected him. When he heard him, he was greatly perplexed; and yet he liked to listen to him. [21]But an opportunity came when Herod on his birthday gave a banquet for his courtiers and officers and for the leaders of Galilee. [22]When his daughter Herodias came in and danced, she pleased Herod and his guests; and the king said to the girl, "Ask me for whatever you wish, and I will give it." [23]And he solemnly swore to her, "Whatever you ask me, I will give you, even half of my kingdom." [24]She went out and said to her mother, "What should I ask for?" She replied, "The head of John the baptizer." [25]Immediately she rushed back to the king and requested, "I want you to give me at once the head of John the Baptist on a platter." [26]The king was deeply grieved; yet out of regard for

his oaths and for the guests, he did not want to refuse her. [27]Immediately the king sent a soldier of the guard with orders to bring John's head. He went and beheaded him in the prison, [28]brought his head on a platter, and gave it to the girl. Then the girl gave it to her mother. [29]When his disciples heard about it, they came and took his body, and laid it in a tomb.

Reflection

This episode with King Herod, also known in history as Herod Antipas, is similar to many Bible stories that start out with a vision that came in a dream. Though Herod is by no means the only bad actor in the story, his unsavory behavior is difficult to ignore. Describing the birthday festivities, Saint Ambrose of Milan (c. 333-397) referred to it as "A banquet of death...set out with royal luxury..."* It is entirely possible that Herod actually saw in a dream that the man whom he had murdered by decapitation had been raised from the dead in the person of Jesus to come back and torment him once again. If so, that must have been one doozy of a nightmare!

This story is one of an ultimate contrast between Herod the successful and John the significant. If ever we needed an example of success at any price, this episode of Herod's unrestrained ambition gives it to us. In comparison, John was a man of significant faith who lived his life to the very end faithful to the God who had called him.

Though the contrast between success and significance is easily overstated, nevertheless it is a contrast which followers of Christ Jesus will be well served to remember and hold in tension.

*Ancient Christian Commentary on Scripture: New Testament II–Mark, Eds. Thomas Oden and Christopher Hall (Downers Grove, IL: InterVarsity, 1998, p. 85).

The Rt. Rev. James B. Magness
Bishop Suffragan for the
Armed Forces and Federal Ministries
Washington, DC

Questions

If another person, perhaps a friend or a coworker, were asked to tell the story of your life, would they describe you as having been in pursuit of success or significance? Why and how?

Prayer

Gracious God, in the midst of our busy lives we pray for your Holy Spirit to remain with us always. Give us the clarity of mind to see and choose significance as we serve your people, through your Son our Savior Jesus Christ, our one true Lord. *Amen.*

Mark 6:30-44

³⁰The apostles gathered around Jesus, and told him all that they had done and taught. ³¹He said to them, "Come away to a deserted place all by yourselves and rest a while." For many were coming and going, and they had no leisure even to eat. ³²And they went away in the boat to a deserted place by themselves. ³³Now many saw them going and recognized them, and they hurried there on foot from all the towns and arrived ahead of them. ³⁴As he went ashore, he saw a great crowd; and he had compassion for them, because they were like sheep without a shepherd; and he began to teach them many things. ³⁵When it grew late, his disciples came to him and said, "This is a deserted place, and the hour is now very late; ³⁶send them away so that they may go into the surrounding country and villages and buy something for themselves to eat." ³⁷But he answered them, "You give them something to eat." They said to him, "Are we to go and buy two hundred denarii worth of bread, and give it to them to eat?" ³⁸And he said to them, "How many loaves have you? Go and see." When they had found out, they said, "Five, and two fish." ³⁹Then he ordered them to get all the people to sit down in groups on the green grass. ⁴⁰So they sat down in groups of hundreds and of fifties. ⁴¹Taking the five loaves and the two fish, he looked up to heaven, and blessed and broke the loaves, and gave them to his disciples to set before the people; and he divided the two fish among them all. ⁴²And all ate and were filled; ⁴³and they took up twelve baskets full of broken pieces and of the fish. ⁴⁴Those who had eaten the loaves numbered five thousand men.

Reflection

The disciples are excited about the success of their ministry, and they cannot wait to share their stories with Jesus. Those gathered around Jesus are called apostles (meaning "those who are sent"). One might think that Jesus would send these apostles straight back out into the mission field, fueled by their passion for the gospel. Instead, we find Jesus inviting them away to a deserted place to pray, perhaps the beginning of the first Christian retreat. But they don't get very far. We are told that the crowds follow them, and, to the annoyance of the disciples, Jesus doesn't make the crowds wait but sits thousands of them down and feeds them.

Notice that Jesus isn't angry with the crowds for interrupting his time of prayer with the disciples. Instead he has compassion on them and meets them where they are. While the disciples are anxious at the interruption and are concerned about their own hunger, Jesus offers a non-anxious presence to both the people and the disciples and gives to each sustenance for the journey. Similar to the disciples, we are called by Jesus away from the busyness of our lives and into prayer. And similar to the disciples, we can be left anxious and even angry as the demands of our lives can crash into these times. Thanks be to God that in the silence and the busyness, God meets us where we are and offers compassion and love.

The Rev. Jennifer Strawbridge
Chaplain and Fellow at Keble College
Oxford, England

Questions

Where do you find spaces of prayer and quiet to spend time with God each day?

What part of your day is devoted to prayer and to sustaining relationships in a way that realistically takes into account your situation and the demands placed upon you?

Prayer

Increase my faith, O Lord; give me diligence to learn and understand the gospel; open my heart to trust you; let my doubts spur me to seek deeper understanding with patience; for you have given me a mind to question, time to grow and mature, and you call me to know, to love, and to serve you even in the midst of uncertainty. *Amen.*

—*Saint Augustine's Prayer Book*

Mark 6:45-56

⁴⁵Immediately he made his disciples get into the boat and go on ahead to the other side, to Bethsaida, while he dismissed the crowd. ⁴⁶After saying farewell to them, he went up on the mountain to pray.

⁴⁷When evening came, the boat was out on the sea, and he was alone on the land. ⁴⁸When he saw that they were straining at the oars against an adverse wind, he came towards them early in the morning, walking on the sea. He intended to pass them by. ⁴⁹But when they saw him walking on the sea, they thought it was a ghost and cried out; ⁵⁰for they all saw him and were terrified. But immediately he spoke to them and said, "Take heart, it is I; do not be afraid." ⁵¹Then he got into the boat with them and the wind ceased. And they were utterly astounded, ⁵²for they did not understand about the loaves, but their hearts were hardened.

⁵³When they had crossed over, they came to land at Gennesaret and moored the boat. ⁵⁴When they got out of the boat, people at once recognized him, ⁵⁵and rushed about that whole region and began to bring the sick on mats to wherever they heard he was. ⁵⁶And wherever he went, into villages or cities or farms, they laid the sick in the marketplaces, and begged him that they might touch even the fringe of his cloak; and all who touched it were healed.

Reflection

The Sea of Galilee figures significantly in the stories of Jesus and his ministry. He spends much time with his disciples on its waters; it is the one place where distance from the crowds is guaranteed. In this story, the disciples have just witnessed the feeding of thousands of people, and yet, as in much of Mark's Gospel, they still do not understand who Jesus is. And, as Jesus finally claims some time alone to pray, the disciples are caught in a sudden storm.

It's a curious story since Jesus sees them in trouble and walks out on the water as if to check on them. When he sees they are struggling but not in danger of drowning, we are told he intends to keep walking. He changes his mind, however, when the disciples are filled with fear that he is a ghost. He joins them in the boat, calms the storm, and they continue on their way, with the disciples not able to grasp what has just happened. Maybe they want their feet to be on solid ground before they take it all in. But in the moment, they are so afraid that they fail to notice that Jesus has offered them peace in the midst of the storm. They do not see that the living God is in the chaos with them, not waiting on the shore for them to pull through but meeting them in their fear.

The Rev. Jennifer Strawbridge
Chaplain and Fellow at Keble College
Oxford, England

A Journey with Mark

Question

Reflect on stormy times in your life when you have been fearful. How, in times of fear and chaos, might you be able to receive the peace that only God can give, trusting that God will be with you as you search for solid ground?

Prayer

O God, you have made of one blood all the peoples of the earth, and sent your blessed Son to preach peace to those who are far off and to those who are near: Grant that people everywhere may seek after you and find you, bring the nations into your fold, pour out your Spirit upon all flesh, and hasten the coming of your kingdom; through Jesus Christ our Lord, who lives and reigns with you and the Holy Spirit, one God, now and for ever. Amen.

—*The Book of Common Prayer*

Mark 7:1-13

7 Now when the Pharisees and some of the scribes who had come from Jerusalem gathered around him, ²they noticed that some of his disciples were eating with defiled hands, that is, without washing them. ³(For the Pharisees, and all the Jews, do not eat unless they thoroughly wash their hands, thus observing the tradition of the elders; ⁴and they do not eat anything from the market unless they wash it; and there are also many other traditions that they observe, the washing of cups, pots, and bronze kettles.) ⁵So the Pharisees and the scribes asked him, "Why do your disciples not live according to the tradition of the elders, but eat with defiled hands?" ⁶He said to them, "Isaiah prophesied rightly about you hypocrites, as it is written, 'This people honors me with their lips, but their hearts are far from me; ⁷in vain do they worship me, teaching human precepts as doctrines.' ⁸You abandon the commandment of God and hold to human tradition."

⁹Then he said to them, "You have a fine way of rejecting the commandment of God in order to keep your tradition! ¹⁰For Moses said, 'Honor your father and your mother'; and, 'Whoever speaks evil of father or mother must surely die.' ¹¹But you say that if anyone tells father or mother, 'Whatever support you might have had from me is Corban' (that is, an offering to God)— ¹²then you no longer permit doing anything for a father or mother, ¹³thus making void the word of God through your tradition that you have handed on. And you do many things like this."

Reflection

Here is the polemical Jesus, in your face, a voice with which we are perhaps less familiar, calling people hypocrites to their face. What to make of Jesus' less-than-gentle engagement of the Pharisees?

Consider carefully his critique. The Pharisees are not Jewish enough, in effect. They have forgotten the prophetic instructions of Isaiah. They have allowed their hearts to wander, being too impressed with human teaching. They have taken their eyes off of God.

Jesus is not anti-Jewish, as if Christianity were about overcoming inherent limitations and faults of Judaism. Yet much of Christian history has assumed this very thing: that Christianity leaves the Jewish God and Jewish teaching behind. If we think this way, the Old Testament will seem foreign, and we paradoxically will be farther away from comprehending Jesus and his teaching.

Jesus advises a return to Moses. Revere again, he says, the Word of God, which is the real tradition. That is, devote yourself to the Old Testament scriptures as your own, in order to understand them rightly. Meditate on the commandments of God.

Amazingly, the Word of God propounds God's holy word. For this reason, the Christian Church treasures these same sacred scriptures. Continuity with the past is our rule, propounded by Jesus himself, who incarnates fulfillment. "If you believed Moses, you would believe me, for he wrote about me. But if you do not believe what he wrote, how will you believe what I say?" (John 5:46-47).

Christopher Wells
Executive Director and Editor,
Living Church Foundation
Milwaukee, Wisconsin

Question

Read Luke 18:9-14. Is it possible to avoid Pharisaism without falling into pharisaical self-righteousness—thanking God that we are not like those fussy, legalistic Pharisees?

Prayer

Lord, you have called your Church from all nations and peoples, starting with the seed of Abraham. Teach us to understand the good news in all of scripture, which you have revealed through your Son, our Lord Jesus Christ. *Amen.*

Mark 7:14-23

¹⁴Then he called the crowd again and said to them, "Listen to me, all of you, and understand: ¹⁵there is nothing outside a person that by going in can defile, but the things that come out are what defile."

¹⁷When he had left the crowd and entered the house, his disciples asked him about the parable. ¹⁸He said to them, "Then do you also fail to understand? Do you not see that whatever goes into a person from outside cannot defile, ¹⁹since it enters, not the heart but the stomach, and goes out into the sewer?" (Thus he declared all foods clean.) ²⁰And he said, "It is what comes out of a person that defiles. ²¹For it is from within, from the human heart, that evil intentions come: fornication, theft, murder, ²²adultery, avarice, wickedness, deceit, licentiousness, envy, slander, pride, folly. ²³All these evil things come from within, and they defile a person."

Reflection

"Listen to me, all of you, and understand," says Jesus, the teacher. And he builds again on Old Testament precedents, concerning the rightly ordered heart, mentioned earlier in the chapter with reference to Isaiah. The heart is the seat of the soul. It is what Paul calls the mind: "Let the same mind be in you that was in Christ Jesus" (Philippians 2:5). Several chapters later in Mark, Jesus will show that all three are the same in his famous elaboration on Deuteronomy 6: "You shall love the Lord your God with all your heart, and with all your soul, and with all your mind, and with all your strength" (Mark 12:30). This is an established teaching, Jesus is saying, according to the law and the prophets.

And what is it? How shall we give God our hearts? Jesus' list of vices is important, since it sets forth what we are not to do. If we avoid "these evil things," by God's grace we will do well.

By God's grace. We say this because all have sinned and fallen short of the glory of God (see Romans 3:23). *All* is certainly comprehensive. We can only trust in God's goodness and mercy toward us. God's love is proven despite our faithlessness (Romans 5:8). In the strength of our reconciliation with God, we are able to scrutinize our obedience and strive for sustained faithfulness. This also will be a gift, devoutly to be sought.

Christopher Wells
Executive Director and Editor,
Living Church Foundation
Milwaukee, Wisconsin

A Journey with Mark

Question

Linger for a while on Jesus' long list of vices that climb into our hearts: "fornication, theft, murder, adultery, avarice, wickedness, deceit, licentiousness, envy, slander, pride, folly." Are there any of these of which you might be guilty in some areas of your life?

Prayer

Heavenly Father, we long to be your faithful disciples. Give us grace and strength to see where we fail, and help us to trust in you. Save us from self-reliance, and give us true humility and self-abasement, through your Son, our Lord Jesus Christ. *Amen.*

DAY 21

Mark 7: 24-30

24 From there he set out and went away to the region of Tyre. He entered a house and did not want anyone to know he was there. Yet he could not escape notice, 25 but a woman whose little daughter had an unclean spirit immediately heard about him, and she came and bowed down at his feet. 26 Now the woman was a Gentile, of Syrophoenician origin. She begged him to cast the demon out of her daughter. 27 He said to her, "Let the children be fed first, for it is not fair to take the children's food and throw it to the dogs." 28 But she answered him, "Sir, even the dogs under the table eat the children's crumbs." 29 Then he said to her, "For saying that, you may go—the demon has left your daughter." 30 So she went home, found the child lying on the bed, and the demon gone.

A Journey with Mark

Reflection

We can only imagine the weight of resistance. It must have been incredibly heavy coming against this mother. A woman. A non-Jew. Gripped by desperation, she relentlessly petitions an exhausted Jesus for her daughter's healing. Can we imagine what the voices inside her head must have been saying? *Oh, he's not a real healer, he can't do anything about your daughter. Besides, she's sick beyond repair, nothing else has been able to heal her, what makes you think Jesus can? And even if he could you're wasting your time thinking he would possibly pay any attention to you.*

Yet there she goes—plowing through the resistance to make her case and win her cause. Facing resistance is the one sure thing you and I can expect whenever we attempt to do the right thing. Whenever we take the risk of following the good voice inside of us, we will find resistance. Think, for example, of the critics, the butterflies, and the thoughts that keep us up at night. These come whenever we try something new, create something novel, stand up for the underdog, authentically give of ourselves, bare our souls to another, and attempt to get real with our lives. Whenever we endeavor to follow the Spirit, we will come up against resistance.

And the Syrophoenician woman reminds us that resistance is the great validator. The naysaying voices actually have a positive effect in assuring us we are onto something—for nothing good is ever easy. This is discipleship. This is the way of Jesus.

The Rev. Chris Yaw
Rector of St. David's Episcopal Church
Founder of ChurchNext
Southfield, Michigan

Questions

What is the resistance you are facing today?

In what ways does your resistance attest to the validity of your endeavor?

Prayer

Almighty God, grant us the wisdom to discern the voices of resistance. Help us bend to the way of your Spirit, and grant us strength to move against powers and principalities that would keep us from being who you want us to be. We ask this in the name of the one who conquered resistance and dwells with you and the Holy Spirit, one God, forever and ever. *Amen.*

DAY 22

Mark 7:31-37

³¹Then he returned from the region of Tyre, and went by way of Sidon towards the Sea of Galilee, in the region of the Decapolis. ³²They brought to him a deaf man who had an impediment in his speech; and they begged him to lay his hand on him. ³³He took him aside in private, away from the crowd, and put his fingers into his ears, and he spat and touched his tongue. ³⁴Then looking up to heaven, he sighed and said to him, "Ephphatha," that is, "Be opened." ³⁵And immediately his ears were opened, his tongue was released, and he spoke plainly. ³⁶Then Jesus ordered them to tell no one; but the more he ordered them, the more zealously they proclaimed it. ³⁷They were astounded beyond measure, saying, "He has done everything well; he even makes the deaf to hear and the mute to speak."

Reflection

I was blind, and I was deaf. When it came to the plight of the Haitians and their ongoing battle against poverty and disease, I was clueless. Then I went to Haiti. My eyes and ears were opened.

I was blind and deaf to the joy and responsibility of fatherhood. How could parents be so fulfilled yet so stressed out? Then I became a dad. My eyes and ears were opened. I was blind and deaf to the plight of the divorced. What was the depth of their pain? Then I got divorced. My eyes and ears were opened. These are humanizing experiences. These are healing experiences.

If you're like me, you may suspect that you spend your days far more blind and deaf than you care to admit. Each day brings mysterious newness filled with far more questions than answers. Yet each day also offers insight and understanding. These revelations come from above, and they come from a God who wants us to be whole.

When Jesus chooses to heal this blind and deaf man, he witnesses to God's desire for us to be healed—to be constantly awakened to what's around us. God wants our eyes and ears opened. God wants us to be able to see that each day offers us a new revelation, a new insight, a path from blindness to sight, from deafness to hearing. It is in deeper awareness that we more fully partake of our God-given humanity. It's the most common way Jesus heals us today.

The Rev. Chris Yaw
Rector of St. David's Episcopal Church
Founder of ChurchNext
Southfield, Michigan

Questions

Think over the past year. In what ways have you been blind and deaf?

In what ways have your eyes and ears been opened?

Prayer

O God of healing power, whose desire is always to bring wholeness: Grant us insight into all that is around us that we may observe your healing power; and equip us to go out into the world as your agents of restoration. Use us to bring healing and wholeness to others; all this we ask in the name of our healer, Jesus Christ our Lord. *Amen.*

DAY 23

Mark 8:1-13

8 In those days when there was again a great crowd without anything to eat, he called his disciples and said to them, ²"I have compassion for the crowd, because they have been with me now for three days and have nothing to eat. ³If I send them away hungry to their homes, they will faint on the way—and some of them have come from a great distance." ⁴His disciples replied, "How can one feed these people with bread here in the desert?" ⁵He asked them, "How many loaves do you have?" They said, "Seven." ⁶Then he ordered the crowd to sit down on the ground; and he took the seven loaves, and after giving thanks he broke them and gave them to his disciples to distribute; and they distributed them to the crowd. ⁷They had also a few small fish; and after blessing them, he ordered that these too should be distributed. ⁸They ate and were filled; and they took up the broken pieces left over, seven baskets full. ⁹Now there were about four thousand people. And he sent them away. ¹⁰And immediately he got into the boat with his disciples and went to the district of Dalmanutha.

¹¹The Pharisees came and began to argue with him, asking him for a sign from heaven, to test him. ¹²And he sighed deeply in his spirit and said, "Why does this generation ask for a sign? Truly I tell you, no sign will be given to this generation." ¹³And he left them, and getting into the boat again, he went across to the other side.

Reflection

In the story of the feeding of the four thousand, Jesus transforms seven loaves of bread and a few small fish into a meal for the multitude. It is not only enough but even more than the people can consume. Although in this case Jesus performs a miracle, elsewhere in the Bible he teaches us (as in the parable of the master allotting talents to the three slaves) that we, too, are called upon to take what we have, even if it is a little, and transform it into abundance for God's kingdom.

Several years ago my son and a group of his high school friends started a microfinance organization that solicited donations and then made loans from the donated funds to individuals in developing countries. As is typical of microfinance, these loans were very small—from several hundred to a few thousand dollars—and generally were made to individuals to grow their small family businesses. My son and his friends chose the individuals to whom the loans were made. In each instance, the students considered not only the need of the particular individual requesting a loan but also the role that individual's business played in his or her broader community. The students were determined to use their limited resources to benefit family businesses that had the potential to fuel other family businesses—and thereby to ensure that a very small sum loaned to one individual could multiply to benefit an entire community.

Mary Kate Wold
CEO and President,
Church Pension Fund
New York, New York

Questions_____

What examples can you think of where someone has created abundance from limited resources for the benefit of God's kingdom?

What opportunities to create abundance are presented to you?

Prayer _____

Gracious God, we thank you and praise you for giving us not only all that we need but also an abundance. Inspire us to multiply the resources and talents you have given us for the benefit of your kingdom. *Amen.*

Mark 8:14-26

[14]Now the disciples had forgotten to bring any bread; and they had only one loaf with them in the boat. [15]And he cautioned them, saying, "Watch out—beware of the yeast of the Pharisees and the yeast of Herod." [16]They said to one another, "It is because we have no bread." [17]And becoming aware of it, Jesus said to them, "Why are you talking about having no bread? Do you still not perceive or understand? Are your hearts hardened? [18]Do you have eyes, and fail to see? Do you have ears, and fail to hear? And do you not remember? [19]When I broke the five loaves for the five thousand, how many baskets full of broken pieces did you collect?" They said to him, "Twelve." [20]"And the seven for the four thousand, how many baskets full of broken pieces did you collect?" And they said to him, "Seven." [21]Then he said to them, "Do you not yet understand?" [22]They came to Bethsaida. Some people brought a blind man to him and begged him to touch him. [23]He took the blind man by the hand and led him out of the village; and when he had put saliva on his eyes and laid his hands on him, he asked him, "Can you see anything?" [24]And the man looked up and said, "I can see people, but they look like trees, walking." [25]Then Jesus laid his hands on his eyes again; and he looked intently and his sight was restored, and he saw everything clearly. [26]Then he sent him away to his home, saying, "Do not even go into the village."

Reflection

This passage raises many questions. Why did Jesus lead the blind man out of the city? Why the saliva? Why didn't the healing work the first time? There have been many theories concerning these questions, and layers of meaning have been read into the facts as told. For example, some say that the two-step process Jesus used to restore sight to the blind man is itself a parable, illustrating that there may be multiple steps to faith, to seeing God clearly, or to perfecting one's faith.

I am sure that Jesus intended layers of meaning to be read into his various actions in healing the blind man. However, I also think there is much to be learned by simply taking the facts at face value. Jesus did not merely give a sign, quickly and efficiently declaring the blind man cured. Rather Jesus himself took the blind man by the hand. He himself led the man out of the city, presumably to a place of relative quiet, comfort, and privacy. Jesus used his own saliva, very possibly to avoid irritating the man's dull eyes when he touched them.

Like a careful and exacting ophthalmologist, Jesus adjusted, tested, and then perfected the man's vision. In these actions, without requiring any deeper analysis, Jesus provided us with a model of tenderness, patience, and compassion. He coupled good works with a caring, human touch, treating another person as truly beloved.

Mary Kate Wold
CEO and President,
Church Pension Fund
New York, New York

Questions

Do you slow down enough to recognize Jesus' tender touch in your life?

Do you ever serve others merely in the spirit of performing a do-good, "check-the-box" deed without following Jesus' example of sincere tenderness, patience, and compassion?

Prayer

Gracious God, we thank you for being a personal God and for treating each of us as beloved. Help us to follow your example by treating our brothers and sisters with heartfelt tenderness, patience, and compassion. *Amen.*

Mark 8:27-38

27 Jesus went on with his disciples to the villages of Caesarea Philippi; and on the way he asked his disciples, "Who do people say that I am?" 28 And they answered him, "John the Baptist; and others, Elijah; and still others, one of the prophets." 29 He asked them, "But who do you say that I am?" Peter answered him, "You are the Messiah." 30 And he sternly ordered them not to tell anyone about him.

31 Then he began to teach them that the Son of Man must undergo great suffering, and be rejected by the elders, the chief priests, and the scribes, and be killed, and after three days rise again. 32 He said all this quite openly. And Peter took him aside and began to rebuke him. 33 But turning and looking at his disciples, he rebuked Peter and said, "Get behind me, Satan! For you are setting your mind not on divine things but on human things."

34 He called the crowd with his disciples, and said to them, "If any want to become my followers, let them deny themselves and take up their cross and follow me. 35 For those who want to save their life will lose it, and those who lose their life for my sake, and for the sake of the gospel, will save it. 36 For what will it profit them to gain the whole world and forfeit their life? 37 Indeed, what can they give in return for their life? 38 Those who are ashamed of me and of my words in this adulterous and sinful generation, of them the Son of Man will also be ashamed when he comes in the glory of his Father with the holy angels."

Reflection

Today's reading is a pivotal moment in the gospel. Peter's declaration about Jesus falls in the exact middle of Mark's Gospel, marking this moment perhaps as the most significant turning point in the disciple's journey with Jesus. In this passage, Jesus is identified as the Christ or the Messiah who will bring about our redemption.

He asks the disciples who people think that he is. They answer, John the Baptist, Elijah, or one of the prophets. Then Jesus asks them, "But who do you say that I am?" This is a question that none of us can evade. Peter boldly replies, "You are the Messiah." This is the response every Christian is called to make, but often it takes many years to reach the point where this truth becomes our truth and this response our response. Truly, this is a day never to forget.

Jesus teaches them that the Son of Man must undergo great suffering, be rejected by the elders, chief priests, and scribes, be killed, and after three days rise again. This is not the kind of lesson that they or we can easily accept. Peter rebukes Jesus for speaking about suffering and death. Like many of Jesus' followers, Peter desires a Messiah who will overthrow the Roman oppressors. Like many of us, he desires a leader who shows no vulnerability and projects only strength and self-assurance. Yet in verse 33 Jesus counters, "Get behind me, Satan! For you are not setting your mind on divine things, but on human things."

God invites us to set our minds on heavenly things, which does not mean merely thinking nice thoughts or striving to enlist God to our side. It means trusting that God often works through vulnerability and weakness rather than through strength and certainty. It calls for believing in heaven, the Holy Trinity, the divinity of Christ, and the Resurrection—our foundational Christian beliefs—and being open to God's will. It is only when we accept these beliefs on faith, surrender ourselves to God's will, and realize that God transforms weakness and despair into glory and hope that we truly begin to make progress on the Christian journey.

The Rev. Marek P. Zabriskie
Rector of St. Thomas' Episcopal Church
Founder of The Bible Challenge
Fort Washington, Pennsylvania

Questions_____

Who is Jesus for you? Is he the Christ or the Messiah?

What key Christian beliefs are most challenging for you to accept?

How have you encountered God through weakness and vulnerability?

Prayer _____

Gracious God, you love us throughout our Christian journey, where our faith ebbs and flows like the ocean tides. Help us to strengthen and deepen our sense of faith so that we might serve you faithfully as you invite us to walk beside you on the road to Jerusalem. *Amen.*

Mark 9:1-13

9 And he said to them, "Truly I tell you, there are some standing here who will not taste death until they see that the kingdom of God has come with power."

²Six days later, Jesus took with him Peter and James and John, and led them up a high mountain apart, by themselves. And he was transfigured before them, ³and his clothes became dazzling white, such as no one on earth could bleach them. ⁴And there appeared to them Elijah with Moses, who were talking with Jesus. ⁵Then Peter said to Jesus, "Rabbi, it is good for us to be here; let us make three dwellings, one for you, one for Moses, and one for Elijah." ⁶He did not know what to say, for they were terrified. ⁷Then a cloud overshadowed them, and from the cloud there came a voice, "This is my Son, the Beloved; listen to him!" ⁸Suddenly when they looked around, they saw no one with them any more, but only Jesus.

⁹As they were coming down the mountain, he ordered them to tell no one about what they had seen, until after the Son of Man had risen from the dead. ¹⁰So they kept the matter to themselves, questioning what this rising from the dead could mean. ¹¹Then they asked him, "Why do the scribes say that Elijah must come first?" ¹²He said to them, "Elijah is indeed coming first to restore all things. How then is it written about the Son of Man, that he is to go through many sufferings and be treated with contempt? ¹³But I tell you that Elijah has come, and they did to him whatever they pleased, as it is written about him."

Reflection

The story of the Transfiguration is perhaps my favorite Bible story. It offers a window into Jesus' divinity and has inspired one of the greatest celebrations of the Orthodox Church. Jesus leads his closest friends—Peter, James, and John—on a hike up a mountain. Some say they climbed Mount Tabor, but other scholars speculate that it was Mount Hermon, located fourteen miles from Caesarea Philippi and towering 11,000 feet above the Jordan valley.

Jesus is transfigured in a scene reminiscent of Exodus, where "… the cloud covered [Mount Sinai] for six days; on the seventh day [the LORD] called to Moses out of the cloud" (Exodus 24:16). Jesus speaks with Moses, the law giver, and Elijah, the prophet who Jews believe to this day will return before the messiah comes. The Transfiguration is a theophany and a mystical event. Peter offers to construct a house so the disciples can remain with Jesus, Moses, and Elijah. Epiphanies like this, however, are fleeting gifts from God that cannot be captured. They transform us and pass but leave us forever changed.

Mark alone adds that Jesus' clothes "…became dazzling white, such as no one on earth could bleach them." Truly, this is a miraculous moment, where God lifts the veil and allows the disciples to see that they are in the presence of the Glory of God, the Messiah.

A cloud overshadows them, and God speaks. So often when dark clouds overshadow us, God speaks most clearly. When the world around us seems darkest, we must trust that God is doing something extraordinary in our lives. Moses' encounter with God on Mount Sinai and Jesus' Transfiguration motivated the anonymous author of *The Cloud of Unknowing* to write his fourteenth-century spiritual classic on prayer, which in turn inspired the centering prayer movement.

After having a mountaintop experience one day and experiencing a profound closeness with God while hiking on Mount Desert Island, Bishop William Reed Huntington, a great figure of The Episcopal Church, returned home. There he penned the prayer that we recite each August 6, when we celebrate the feast of the Transfiguration.

The Rev. Marek P. Zabriskie
Rector of St. Thomas' Episcopal Church
Founder of The Bible Challenge
Fort Washington, Pennsylvania

Questions

What have been your spiritual mountaintop experiences?

Can you trust that when dark clouds hover over your life, God will still speak to you? Are you able to listen?

I know He is with me in every dark time I've had but even if He is speaking to me I don't think I hear a word cuz I'm wrapped up in myself!

Prayer

O God, who on the holy mount revealed to chosen witnesses your well-beloved Son, wonderfully transfigured, in raiment white and glistening: Mercifully grant that we, being delivered from the disquietude of this world, may by faith behold the King in his beauty; who with you, O Father, and you, O Holy Spirit, lives and reigns, one God, for ever and ever. *Amen.*

— Collect for the Feast of the Transfiguration
The Book of Common Prayer

Day 27

Mark 9:14-32

[14]When they came to the
disciples, they saw a great crowd
around them, and some scribes
arguing with them. [15]When
the whole crowd saw him, they
were immediately overcome
with awe, and they ran forward
to greet him. [16]He asked them,
"What are you arguing about
with them?" [17]Someone from the
crowd answered him, "Teacher,
I brought you my son; he has a
spirit that makes him unable to
speak; [18]and whenever it seizes
him, it dashes him down; and he
foams and grinds his teeth and
becomes rigid; and I asked your
disciples to cast it out, but they
could not do so." [19]He answered
them, "You faithless generation,
how much longer must I be
among you? How much longer
must I put up with you? Bring
him to me." [20]And they brought
the boy to him. When the
spirit saw him, immediately it
convulsed the boy, and he fell
on the ground and rolled about,
foaming at the mouth. [21]Jesus
asked the father, "How long has
this been happening to him?"
And he said, "From childhood.
[22]It has often cast him into
the fire and into the water,
to destroy him; but if you are
able to do anything, have pity
on us and help us." [23]Jesus said
to him, "If you are able! —All
things can be done for the one
who believes." [24]Immediately
the father of the child cried out,
"I believe; help my unbelief!"
[25]When Jesus saw that a crowd
came running together, he
rebuked the unclean spirit,
saying to it, "You spirit that
keeps this boy from speaking
and hearing, I command you,
come out of him, and never
enter him again!" [26]After crying
out and convulsing him terribly,
it came out, and the boy was

like a corpse, so that most of them said, "He is dead." ²⁷But Jesus took him by the hand and lifted him up, and he was able to stand. ²⁸When he had entered the house, his disciples asked him privately, "Why could we not cast it out?" ²⁹He said to them, "This kind can come out only through prayer." ³⁰They went on from there and passed through Galilee. He did not want anyone to know it; ³¹for he was teaching his disciples, saying to them, "The Son of Man is to be betrayed into human hands, and they will kill him, and three days after being killed, he will rise again." ³²But they did not understand what he was saying and were afraid to ask him.

Reflection

As a brand new and quite young chaplain for the hospital, I felt incredibly ill-equipped to engage in this type of pastoral work. After a number of awkward bedside conversations, I once again found myself standing next to a gravely ill person and feeling beyond inept. As I began to speak, she raised her hand and said, "Chaplain, I am praying. Why don't you sit down over there and quietly join me?" This transformative experience was the beginning of my understanding of prayerful pastoral presence.

I always return to that prayerful encounter when I read and reflect on this passage from Mark. We learn about Jesus as he comes upon a challenging situation with the disciples. A crowd has formed around a very sick child whom the disciples are unable to heal. Jesus is clearly disappointed with the disciples for what he calls their lack of faith. Jesus then points out that all things come to those with faith. The desperate father of the boy begs Jesus for that type of belief. And then, in front of a continually disbelieving crowd, Jesus heals the boy.

Jesus talks later with the disciples about the importance of prayer, which will be critical as Jesus once again tries to prepare the disciples for his impending death. And the same is true for us. Like the disciples, we are called by Jesus to a faithfulness centered in prayer.

The Rt. Rev. Brian N. Prior
Bishop of the Episcopal Church in Minnesota
Minneapolis, Minnesota

Questions

What prayer do you pray when you find yourself in a challenging situation?

How can you offer a "prayerful pastoral presence?"

Prayer

O Lord Jesus Christ, you not only taught but also modeled for your disciples the importance of living a life of prayer. Grant us the wisdom to bring forth all the cares and concerns of our lives and the lives of those we encounter to you in prayer. All this we ask in your name, for you reign one with the Father and Holy Spirit, one God now and forever. *Amen.*

Mark 9:33-49

[33]Then they came to Capernaum; and when he was in the house he asked them, "What were you arguing about on the way?" [34]But they were silent, for on the way they had argued with one another who was the greatest. [35]He sat down, called the twelve, and said to them, "Whoever wants to be first must be last of all and servant of all." [36]Then he took a little child and put it among them; and taking it in his arms, he said to them, [37]"Whoever welcomes one such child in my name welcomes me, and whoever welcomes me welcomes not me but the one who sent me."

[38]John said to him, "Teacher, we saw someone casting out demons in your name, and we tried to stop him, because he was not following us." [39]But Jesus said, "Do not stop him; for no one who does a deed of power in my name will be able soon afterward to speak evil of me. [40]Whoever is not against us is for us. [41]For truly I tell you, whoever gives you a cup of water to drink because you bear the name of Christ will by no means lose the reward.

[42]"If any of you put a stumbling block before one of these little ones who believe in me, it would be better for you if a great millstone were hung around your neck and you were thrown into the sea. [43]If your hand causes you to stumble, cut it off; it is better for you to enter life maimed than to have two hands and to go to hell, to the unquenchable fire. [45]And if your foot causes you to stumble, cut it off; it is better for you to enter life lame than to have two feet and to be thrown into hell.

[47]And if your eye causes you to stumble, tear it out; it is better for you to enter the kingdom of God with one eye than to have two eyes and to be thrown into hell, [48]where their worm never dies, and the fire is never quenched.

[49]"For everyone will be salted with fire.

Reflection

One of the most challenging dynamics I encountered as a camp director was helping the staff understand their role and relationship with the campers. For most staff members, this was their first opportunity in a leadership position. Inevitably, at the beginning of their tenure, they relished in lording over their campers as if the campers were there to serve the staff.

This passage from Mark was incredibly instructive in helping the staff clearly understand their ministry. Jesus comes upon the disciples engaged in a very heated debate. The topic of their discourse is disturbing enough to Jesus that he finds it important to not only correct their errant ways but also to help them truly understand their role and relationship with him. Erroneously, the disciples assume that their closeness to Jesus has bestowed upon them certain heavenly privileges. Jesus quickly and graphically clarifies that following him does not grant them greater privilege but rather demands greater servanthood.

Each of us, regardless of our role or position, has the opportunity to use our gifts each day to serve others just as Jesus modeled for us. That, in the end, is the real privilege.

The Rt. Rev. Brian N. Prior
Bishop of the Episcopal Church in Minnesota
Minneapolis, Minnesota

A Journey with Mark

Questions _____

What are the situations in which you truly feel called to be a servant?

What kind of qualities are important in a servant leader?

Prayer _____

Almighty and everlasting God, through the power of the Holy Spirit you have bestowed upon your people gifts for your service. Embolden us with strength and courage to follow in the way of your son, our Savior Jesus Christ, and to truly live as your loving servants. *Amen.*

Mark 10:1-12

10 He left that place and went to the region of Judea and beyond the Jordan. And crowds again gathered around him; and, as was his custom, he again taught them.

²Some Pharisees came, and to test him they asked, "Is it lawful for a man to divorce his wife?" ³He answered them, "What did Moses command you?" ⁴They said, "Moses allowed a man to write a certificate of dismissal and to divorce her." ⁵But Jesus said to them, "Because of your hardness of heart he wrote this commandment for you. ⁶But from the beginning of creation, 'God made them male and female.' ⁷'For this reason a man shall leave his father and mother and be joined to his wife, ⁸and the two shall become one flesh.' So they are no longer two, but one flesh. ⁹Therefore what God has joined together, let no one separate."

¹⁰Then in the house the disciples asked him again about this matter. ¹¹He said to them, "Whoever divorces his wife and marries another commits adultery against her; ¹²and if she divorces her husband and marries another, she commits adultery."

Reflection

This is one of those disturbing passages in the gospels, one that most of us would prefer to ignore. There seem to be no soft edges in Jesus' reply to the Pharisees who are trying to trip him up. I have been married for almost sixty years so this is scarcely a burning issue for me personally. But as a priest whose chief work is pastoral care, the issue of divorce confronts me almost daily. And as a woman with children, nieces, nephews, and friends of all ages, the stability of marriage remains for me an important issue. When I officiate at weddings, I am always awed and a bit frightened when I intone, "Those whom God has joined together let no one put asunder."

So I am prepared to argue with Jesus. First of all, the historical context: in Biblical times marriage was rarely or perhaps never a romantic arrangement. I can't recall any stories of such free choice as boy and girl meet, they fall in love, and live happily ever after. Nor can I recall a story when the woman, in a time of patriarchy, takes the lead in the courtship.

And we all know marriages that are tragic—instances of ongoing infidelity, domestic abuse, seemingly total breakdown—when suffering has become the work of daily life and when prayer, pastoral care, and professional counseling have not helped. It is almost a cliché, but inevitably I ask myself: What would Jesus do, Jesus the God of tenderness and compassion?

The Rev. Margaret Guenther
Author and Professor Emerita,
The General Theological Seminary
Washington, DC

Question _____

Maybe the vital words in this passage are these: "What God has joined together, let no one separate." When we reflect on marriage, the vital question is where is God, the God of love and fidelity, in the picture. Where is God at the heart of your relationships?

Prayer _____

Loving God, help us to make wise decisions. Help us to grow daily in compassion, to recognize our own imperfection, and humbly to seek your guidance and help. Help us to recognize and remember that our lives are in your hands and that you love us and care for us in our human frailty. *Amen.*

Mark 10:13-31

[13]People were bringing little children to him in order that he might touch them; and the disciples spoke sternly to them. [14]But when Jesus saw this, he was indignant and said to them, "Let the little children come to me; do not stop them; for it is to such as these that the kingdom of God belongs. [15]Truly I tell you, whoever does not receive the kingdom of God as a little child will never enter it." [16]And he took them up in his arms, laid his hands on them, and blessed them.

[17]As he was setting out on a journey, a man ran up and knelt before him, and asked him, "Good Teacher, what must I do to inherit eternal life?" [18]Jesus said to him, "Why do you call me good? No one is good but God alone. [19]You know the commandments: 'You shall not murder; You shall not commit adultery; You shall not steal; You shall not bear false witness; You shall not defraud; Honor your father and mother.'" [20]He said to him, "Teacher, I have kept all these since my youth." [21]Jesus, looking at him, loved him and said, "You lack one thing; go, sell what you own, and give the money to the poor, and you will have treasure in heaven; then come, follow me." [22]When he heard this, he was shocked and went away grieving, for he had many possessions.

[23]Then Jesus looked around and said to his disciples, "How hard it will be for those who have wealth to enter the kingdom of God!" [24]And the disciples were perplexed at these words. But Jesus said to them again, "Children, how hard it is to enter the kingdom of God!

^{25}It is easier for a camel to go through the eye of a needle than for someone who is rich to enter the kingdom of God." ^{26}They were greatly astounded and said to one another, "Then who can be saved?" ^{27}Jesus looked at them and said, "For mortals it is impossible, but not for God; for God all things are possible."

^{28}Peter began to say to him, "Look, we have left everything and followed you." ^{29}Jesus said,

"Truly I tell you, there is no one who has left house or brothers or sisters or mother or father or children or fields, for my sake and for the sake of the good news, ^{30}who will not receive a hundredfold now in this age— houses, brothers and sisters, mothers and children, and fields with persecutions—and in the age to come eternal life. ^{31}But many who are first will be last, and the last will be first."

Reflection

What a fascinating short passage, with just a few confusing words. Could this all have happened in one short encounter?

First there's a tender picture of Jesus, comfortably holding the children and talking to them in a gentle voice. Maybe he asks them questions and listens to theirs. Maybe he tells them stories—maybe funny stories and then laughs with them. Maybe he sings childlike songs with them, or they simply enjoy sacred time together.

We can learn a lot from these few verses—as parents, grandparents, teachers, and ordinary folk who encounter children in our parish, at the pediatrician's office, on the playground, and at the grocery store. And to our surprise, we may learn what a rich experience this can be—for the child and even more powerfully for us!

But then the abrupt switch to one of the most challenging, awe-inspiring bits of scripture. This anonymous man asks the ultimate question: "What must I do to be saved?" Where has that gentle, permissive Jesus gone? The seeker's reaction may well have been shock. He might have wished that he'd never asked the question.

Perhaps especially those of us with modest needs and acquisitions are surprised at this command that leaves no room for excuses or negotiation. Even those of us who feel our commitment is total want to pretend that Jesus didn't really mean this command—one which I, for one, have never managed to follow. But I hope that my ongoing wish to negotiate will buy me time.

The Rev. Margaret Guenther
Author and Professor Emerita,
The General Theological Seminary
Washington, DC

Question

How can we, hard-working and living in a time and place where even the poor are well off by world standards, respond to Jesus' command?

What is Jesus telling us about our relationship with children and, by extension, with the helpless, hurting, and vulnerable in our lives? Are we capable of suspending judgment and freely offering patience and gentleness?

Prayer

Loving Jesus, help us to be more like you in the small things of our lives. Help us to be gentle and patient, especially with the vulnerable: the children, the aged, the damaged, all who rely on us for care. And help us to see this as joyfully following in your steps, one of the great joys in our imperfect lives. *Amen.*

Mark 10:32-52

[32]They were on the road, going up to Jerusalem, and Jesus was walking ahead of them; they were amazed, and those who followed were afraid. He took the twelve aside again and began to tell them what was to happen to him, [33]saying, "See, we are going up to Jerusalem, and the Son of Man will be handed over to the chief priests and the scribes, and they will condemn him to death; then they will hand him over to the Gentiles; [34]they will mock him, and spit upon him, and flog him, and kill him; and after three days he will rise again."

[35]James and John, the sons of Zebedee, came forward to him and said to him, "Teacher, we want you to do for us whatever we ask of you." [36]And he said to them, "What is it you want me to do for you?" [37]And they said to him, "Grant us to sit, one at your right hand and one at your left, in your glory." [38]But Jesus said to them, "You do not know what you are asking. Are you able to drink the cup that I drink, or be baptized with the baptism that I am baptized with?" [39]They replied, "We are able." Then Jesus said to them, "The cup that I drink you will drink; and with the baptism with which I am baptized, you will be baptized; [40]but to sit at my right hand or at my left is not mine to grant, but it is for those for whom it has been prepared."

[41]When the ten heard this, they began to be angry with James and John. [42]So Jesus called them and said to them, "You know that among the Gentiles those whom they recognize as their rulers lord it over them, and

their great ones are tyrants over them. ⁴³But it is not so among you; but whoever wishes to become great among you must be your servant, ⁴⁴and whoever wishes to be first among you must be slave of all. ⁴⁵For the Son of Man came not to be served but to serve, and to give his life a ransom for many." ⁴⁶They came to Jericho. As he and his disciples and a large crowd were leaving Jericho, Bartimaeus son of Timaeus, a blind beggar, was sitting by the roadside. ⁴⁷When he heard that it was Jesus of Nazareth, he began to shout out and say, "Jesus, Son of David, have mercy on me!" ⁴⁸Many sternly ordered him to be quiet, but he cried out even more loudly, "Son of David, have mercy on me!" ⁴⁹Jesus stood still and said, "Call him here." And they called the blind man, saying to him, "Take heart; get up, he is calling you." ⁵⁰So throwing off his cloak, he sprang up and came to Jesus. ⁵¹Then Jesus said to him, "What do you want me to do for you?" The blind man said to him, "My teacher, let me see again." ⁵²Jesus said to him, "Go; your faith has made you well." Immediately he regained his sight and followed him on the way.

Reflection

While my children were teenagers, I learned that some of the best conversations happen when you are traveling. You can't escape from each other, and the sense of a shared journey encourages shared views. In the car, on a walk, in an airport lounge—or in the case of Jesus and his disciples, on the journey toward all that awaited them in Jerusalem, that center of secular and religious power. The topic of power is at the heart of the conversations. It's preoccupying the disciples, and it lies behind the nationalistic title of "Son of David" shouted by Bartimaeus.

In response we hear Jesus ask the wonderfully penetrating question: "What do you want me to do for you?" This isn't Jesus promising to be all-powerful. He doesn't claim to be able to deliver what is demanded. Indeed with James and John he specifically says he can't meet their flawed expectations. Yet by asking this powerful question he invites hungry disciples and a desperate Bartimaeus to look beyond their ambition or neediness to what they truly long for God to do for them. Becoming great is not on offer. He tells them that the sign of a Christian is not success but sacrifice and brokenness, a shocking or foolish thought to both their contemporaries and ours. Yet what results if we trust in the power of God is the healing of body, heart, and spirit, even on the most difficult of roads.

The Very Rev. June Osborne
Dean of Salisbury
Salisbury, England

Question

Imagine walking with Jesus and having him ask you that same question: "What do you want me to do for you?" How would you answer?

Then imagine Jesus asking it again: "What do you really want me to do for you?"

Prayer

Lord God, you know how influenced we are by symbols of power, by wealth, celebrity, and public opinion. Give us such confidence in your loving way of service that we might know our own hearts better and seek from you the things that lead us into life and liberty. *Amen.*

Mark 11:1-11

11 When they were approaching Jerusalem, at Bethphage and Bethany, near the Mount of Olives, he sent two of his disciples ²and said to them, "Go into the village ahead of you, and immediately as you enter it, you will find tied there a colt that has never been ridden; untie it and bring it. ³If anyone says to you, 'Why are you doing this?' just say this, 'The Lord needs it and will send it back here immediately.'" ⁴They went away and found a colt tied near a door, outside in the street. As they were untying it, ⁵some of the bystanders said to them, "What are you doing, untying the colt?" ⁶They told them what Jesus had said; and they allowed them to take it.

⁷Then they brought the colt to Jesus and threw their cloaks on it; and he sat on it. ⁸Many people spread their cloaks on the road, and others spread leafy branches that they had cut in the fields. ⁹Then those who went ahead and those who followed were shouting, "Hosanna! Blessed is the one who comes in the name of the Lord!

¹⁰ Blessed is the coming kingdom of our ancestor David!

Hosanna in the highest heaven!"

¹¹Then he entered Jerusalem and went into the temple; and when he had looked around at everything, as it was already late, he went out to Bethany with the twelve.

Reflection

One strong image can make more of an impression than a whole library full of words. When Archbishop Desmond Tutu was a boy, he remembers Anglican Bishop Trevor Huddleston raising his hat as a gesture of respect to his mother, a poor black woman. In a single gesture, young Desmond's view of the Church and the attractiveness of the Christian faith were transformed. In the early days of his papacy, Pope Francis spontaneously released a white dove from a cage as he mixed with the crowds in Rome and gave us a symbol of setting things free.

So it was for the people who crowded into Jerusalem for that Passover festival when Jesus chose a donkey as his preferred means of transport. What did they see? Mark believed that Jesus orchestrated a demonstration of lowly kingship, a declaration of the coming kingdom of God. He tells us that no sooner had Jesus arrived than he immediately returned to Bethany. Jesus' purpose was to give the people an image they would not forget. It challenged those who comfortably inhabited the seats of power and those who wished to renegotiate that power by means of force. Jesus wishes to change our mind. Giving us a parable in action, he shows that the ultimate courage is to love deeply and to surrender all we are to what we believe. Like a hat being doffed or a bird released, this man on a donkey changed how the world was seen and understood.

The Very Rev. June Osborne
Dean of Salisbury
Salisbury, England

A Journey with Mark

Question

Has a symbolic gesture or a surprising image stayed with you and shaped your thinking?

How might you change something you do in order to communicate better what you believe?

Prayer

Heavenly Father, open our eyes to see the world in which we live as you see it, and so make us able to live according to your justice and ways of peace. May we hope to change the way others see themselves by our gestures of loving kindness and respect. In your Name we pray. *Amen.*

Mark 11:12-19

¹²On the following day, when they came from Bethany, he was hungry. ¹³Seeing in the distance a fig tree in leaf, he went to see whether perhaps he would find anything on it. When he came to it, he found nothing but leaves, for it was not the season for figs. ¹⁴He said to it, "May no one ever eat fruit from you again." And his disciples heard it.

¹⁵Then they came to Jerusalem. And he entered the temple and began to drive out those who were selling and those who were buying in the temple, and he overturned the tables of the money changers and the seats of those who sold doves; ¹⁶and he would not allow anyone to carry anything through the temple. ¹⁷He was teaching and saying, "Is it not written, 'My house shall be called a house of prayer for all the nations'? But you have made it a den of robbers."

¹⁸And when the chief priests and the scribes heard it, they kept looking for a way to kill him; for they were afraid of him, because the whole crowd was spellbound by his teaching. ¹⁹And when evening came, Jesus and his disciples went out of the city.

Reflection

There is an amazing depth to the Holy Scriptures. Often what we read on the surface barely touches the message. Verse 12 simply says that when Jesus came to Bethany he was hungry, and that in the distance he saw a fig tree in full leaf. Since it was not the season for figs, he went up to inspect the tree to see if there was anything on it. The tree, with all its leaves from a distance, was actually barren. It made a promise it could not keep, hence Jesus' words, "May no one ever eat fruit from you again." His disciples heard him.

What was true of the fig tree was true of the temple. Josephus records that the entire façade of the temple—a complex equal to thirty-five football fields—was covered with gold plate. The upper part was pure white marble and gold spikes lined the roof. The inside was equally impressive. This was to be an outward and visible sign of God's blessing.

When Jesus drove out the money changers, it was not an effort to reform financial abuse. He said, "Is it not written, my house shall be called a house of prayer for all nations? But you have made it a den of robbers." He was referring to another problem: the temple had become a nationalist fortress over and against the nations as opposed to being the focal point of God's mission to the whole world.

The Rt. Rev. Edward L. Salmon Jr.
Dean and President,
Nashotah House Theological Seminary
Milwaukee, Wisconsin

Question

As the crucified and resurrected Lord sitting at the right hand of the Father looks at his Church today and us as his disciples, what does he see?

Some good - devout worshipers, sincere preacher
Some bad - jealousy, quarelling, seekers of power
Some sad - many empty pews - few children.

Prayer

Most merciful God, by the power of your Holy Spirit, help us in your Church to handle the holy things you have given us so that their beauty is manifested not in appearances, but in transformed lives and mercy for the world for which you died. In Jesus' name. *Amen.*

Mark 11:20-33

20In the morning as they passed by, they saw the fig tree withered away to its roots. 21Then Peter remembered and said to him, "Rabbi, look! The fig tree that you cursed has withered." 22Jesus answered them, "Have faith in God. 23Truly I tell you, if you say to this mountain, 'Be taken up and thrown into the sea,' and if you do not doubt in your heart, but believe that what you say will come to pass, it will be done for you. 24So I tell you, whatever you ask for in prayer, believe that you have received it, and it will be yours.

25"Whenever you stand praying, forgive, if you have anything against anyone; so that your Father in heaven may also forgive you your trespasses." 27Again they came to Jerusalem. As he was walking in the temple, the chief priests, the scribes, and the elders came to him 28and said, "By what authority are you doing these things? Who gave you this authority to do them?" 29Jesus said to them, "I will ask you one question; answer me, and I will tell you by what authority I do these things. 30Did the baptism of John come from heaven, or was it of human origin? Answer me." 31They argued with one another, "If we say, 'From heaven,' he will say, 'Why then did you not believe him?' 32But shall we say, 'Of human origin'?" — they were afraid of the crowd, for all regarded John as truly a prophet. 33So they answered Jesus, "We do not know." And Jesus said to them, "Neither will I tell you by what authority I am doing these things."

Reflection

The next day when they passed by, Simon Peter saw the fig tree withered to its roots. He pointed it out to Jesus, who replied, "Truly I tell you, if you say to this mountain, 'Be taken up and thrown into the sea,' and if you do not doubt in your heart, but believe that what you say will come to pass, it will be done for you." This was the mountain in front of them as they journeyed to Jerusalem, the mountain where they were the day before. It was the temple mount that stood for something quite different than the reign of God.

Jesus was inviting his disciples to pray with the same unbending faith he had manifested when he cleansed the temple the day before. The plural "you" suggests corporate requests, not an invitation to individual selfishness. Verse 24 points to God's faithfulness in the presence of deep-seated opposition to the reign of God. If the temple is not immune to God's judgment, then God can be trusted to judge any center of power.

Since the judgment on the temple would not come until its fall in 70 CE, this was the call for an enduring faith that trusts God, who acts through the events of history even if it takes a generation or more. Disciples must remember that oppressed groups can also injure others. When we pray for justice, we must also pray for reconciliation, for reconciliation is the place where justice and forgiveness meet.

When the chief priests, scribes, and elders question the authority of Jesus, he answers a question with a question about John the Baptist. Their answer, "We do not know," highlights his authority.

The Rt. Rev. Edward L. Salmon Jr.
Dean and President,
Nashotah House Theological Seminary
Nashotah, Wisconsin

Questions

Our Lord's statement to have faith in God is an invitation to trust him. Whom and what do we really trust? Is Jesus Lord?

Prayer

Gracious God, as the one who died for us, give us the eyes to see your love for us and the world, that in all the cares of this life, our trust may rest firmly in you. In Jesus' name. *Amen.*

Mark 12:1-17

12 Then he began to speak to them in parables. "A man planted a vineyard, put a fence around it, dug a pit for the wine press, and built a watchtower; then he leased it to tenants and went to another country. [2]When the season came, he sent a slave to the tenants to collect from them his share of the produce of the vineyard. [3]But they seized him, and beat him, and sent him away empty-handed. [4]And again he sent another slave to them; this one they beat over the head and insulted. [5]Then he sent another, and that one they killed. And so it was with many others; some they beat, and others they killed. [6]He had still one other, a beloved son. Finally he sent him to them, saying, 'They will respect my son.' [7]But those tenants said to one another, 'This is the heir; come, let us kill him, and the inheritance will be ours.' [8]So they seized him, killed him, and threw him out of the vineyard. [9]What then will the owner of the vineyard do? He will come and destroy the tenants and give the vineyard to others. [10]Have you not read this scripture:

'The stone that the builders rejected has become the cornerstone; [11]this was the Lord's doing, and it is amazing in our eyes'?"

[12]When they realized that he had told this parable against them, they wanted to arrest him, but they feared the crowd. So they left him and went away.

[13]Then they sent to him some Pharisees and some Herodians to trap him in what he said. [14]And they came and said to him, "Teacher, we know that you are sincere, and show deference to no one; for you

do not regard people with partiality, but teach the way of God in accordance with truth. Is it lawful to pay taxes to the emperor, or not? [15]Should we pay them, or should we not?" But knowing their hypocrisy, he said to them, "Why are you putting me to the test? Bring me a denarius and let me see it." [16]And they brought one. Then he said to them, "Whose head is this, and whose title?" They answered, "The emperor's." [17]Jesus said to them, "Give to the emperor the things that are the emperor's, and to God the things that are God's." And they were utterly amazed at him.

Reflection

Someone once summed up the message of Mark's Gospel in this way: "God gives everything to you. You are to give everything to God. You can't!" At first sight, this doesn't sound much like good news. It presents us with the blank wall of impossibility. One of the reasons the reformers gave for reading the Old Testament was to show that the life it called us to is impossible. One could argue that this is just as true for our reading of the New Testament.

The purpose of these stories is to bring us to the end of our rope, to show us that we aren't up to the task, and to ground us in the life of grace. We look at the world and wonder how we're going to stay together as a human family. Are we going to make it, given our tendency to violence, betrayal, and selfishness? Reading this story about the man who planted a vineyard is a way for us to get in touch with what really matters. Think about what happens to the rightful heir. He is murdered! The story turns our values upside down, revealing the shabbiness and shallowness of much of what we hold dear. We are faced with our inability or unwillingness to see the difference between Caesar and God and thereby to discern the true source of life.

It's no wonder that we want a life where we come out on top. Here we have a core gospel principle: the stone that the builders rejected has become the chief cornerstone. Jesus reveals a God whose power is manifested in self-giving and self-emptying. When we catch a glimpse of the true nature of power, all things are possible with God.

The Very Rev. Alan Jones
Dean Emeritus,
Grace Cathedral, San Francisco
San Francisco, California

A Journey with Mark

Questions _____

What might it mean to be a faithful steward of all that we have been given?

What revolution of values is being stirred up in us to build a community of love and justice?

What might be your next level of surrender to this God who goes to such lengths to bring us home?

Prayer _____

O God, your strangeness continually takes us by surprise! Help us to discern the true nature of power so that we can see the world as you have made it—a gift to be enjoyed and reverenced, shared and celebrated. *Amen.*

Mark 12:18-34

[18]Some Sadducees, who say there is no resurrection, came to him and asked him a question, saying, [19]"Teacher, Moses wrote for us that 'if a man's brother dies, leaving a wife but no child, the man shall marry the widow and raise up children for his brother.' [20]There were seven brothers; the first married and, when he died, left no children; [21]and the second married her and died, leaving no children; and the third likewise; [22]none of the seven left children. Last of all the woman herself died. [23]In the resurrection whose wife will she be? For the seven had married her."

[24]Jesus said to them, "Is not this the reason you are wrong, that you know neither the scriptures nor the power of God? [25]For when they rise from the dead, they neither marry nor are given in marriage, but are like angels in heaven. [26]And as for the dead being raised, have you not read in the book of Moses, in the story about the bush, how God said to him, 'I am the God of Abraham, the God of Isaac, and the God of Jacob'? [27]He is God not of the dead, but of the living; you are quite wrong."

[28]One of the scribes came near and heard them disputing with one another, and seeing that he answered them well, he asked him, "Which commandment is the first of all?" [29]Jesus answered, "The first is, 'Hear, O Israel: the Lord our God, the Lord is one; [30]you shall love the Lord your God with all your heart, and with all your soul, and with all your mind, and with all your strength.' [31]The second is this, 'You shall love your neighbor as yourself.' There is no other

commandment greater than these." [32]Then the scribe said to him, "You are right, Teacher; you have truly said that 'he is one, and besides him there is no other'; [33]and 'to love him with all the heart, and with all the understanding, and with all the strength,' and 'to love one's neighbor as oneself,' —this is much more important than all whole burnt offerings and sacrifices." [34]When Jesus saw that he answered wisely, he said to him, "You are not far from the kingdom of God." After that no one dared to ask him any question.

Reflection

Many of us look at life as a problem to be solved rather than a mystery to be lived. We want clear answers so that questions are finally settled and we can take comfort in knowing that we are right. We also like to know who's in and who's out. The trouble is that we often cannot tell the difference between mere cleverness and true wisdom. We are uncomfortable with the unknown and the unknowable, and we'd rather have a slick answer than live with a probing question. We like to be in the know and be in control.

Saint Augustine tells us, "If you have understood, what you have understood is not God." Much of the journey of faith is in a kind of not knowing, or a letting go of our lust for certainty and learning the risk of trust. The Sadducees in the story, wanting to trap Jesus with their cleverness, come up with a "reasonable" problem to be solved—to show that the promise of resurrection is both false and absurd. They bring to the mystery of faith a literalistic approach to a question that is radically open.

In Jesus we see the adventure of being human is centered on love. The answer to the Sadducees' question lies not in a formulaic approach to life but in appreciation of the centrality of the first commandment. Love trumps everything, especially trick questions about the meaning of life.

The Very Rev. Alan Jones
Dean Emeritus,
Grace Cathedral, San Francisco
San Francisco, California

A Journey with Mark

Questions _____

What kinds of questions are worth asking?

Are you open to a life of faith that deepens questions rather than gives quick and easy answers?

Some say that love trumps everything. Is this true?

Prayer _____

Loving Mystery in whom we live and move and have our being, we give thanks that you continually open our minds with ever-deepening questions and open our hearts to ever greater depths. Help us see in your "deep but dazzling darkness" the love that sustains all things and give us courage to let go of our lust for certainty and embrace the risk of trust. *Amen.*

Mark 12: 35-44

[35]While Jesus was teaching in the temple, he said, "How can the scribes say that the Messiah is the son of David? [36]David himself, by the Holy Spirit, declared, 'The Lord said to my Lord, "Sit at my right hand, until I put your enemies under your feet." '

[37]David himself calls him Lord; so how can he be his son?" And the large crowd was listening to him with delight.

[38]As he taught, he said, "Beware of the scribes, who like to walk around in long robes, and to be greeted with respect in the marketplaces, [39]and to have the best seats in the synagogues and places of honor at banquets! [40]They devour widows' houses and for the sake of appearance say long prayers. They will receive the greater condemnation."

[41]He sat down opposite the treasury, and watched the crowd putting money into the treasury. Many rich people put in large sums. [42]A poor widow came and put in two small copper coins, which are worth a penny. [43]Then he called his disciples and said to them, "Truly I tell you, this poor widow has put in more than all those who are contributing to the treasury. [44]For all of them have contributed out of their abundance; but she out of her poverty has put in everything she had, all she had to live on."

Reflection

What is true teaching and what is faithful living? These questions frame the story known as the widow's mite. The poor woman who quietly gives out of proportion to her means has become a key model of the Christian life. Faithful people, we conclude, give quietly without seeking recognition. Yet the effects of her giving can be seen if one pays attention. She bears witness out of proportion to the amount of the gift.

This teaching highlights Jesus' use of observation and contrast. He observes the official religious leaders of the day and contrasts their demeanor with that of the widow. They offer large sums loudly with expectations of enhancing their status. For them, giving reinforces their authority. By contrast, the poor widow simply gives, trusting that wider benefit will follow, not benefit for herself. There is no reference to her intention, no hint of her personality or her religious faith. For contemporary sensibilities this is frustrating: we cannot probe her motivation. But that is not Jesus' focus.

True teaching, as Jesus embodies, shapes behavior: we are called to act in certain ways. Faithful living may have unclear motives, but one of its marks is sacrificial giving. We who would follow need not become poor, nor are poor people necessarily exalted. A poverty of time or of ability or of self-esteem may be our situation. The point is to give out of who we are and what we have, without seeking reward. Giving becomes its own reward.

The Rev. William L. Sachs, PhD.
Director of the Center for Interfaith Reconciliation,
St. Stephen's Church
Richmond, Virginia

Questions

There is much debate today about being "spiritual" rather than being "religious." What does this passage contribute to the debate?

What is the meaning of being "religious" in this passage?

When and how have you given sacrificially? What does sacrifice in this sense mean to you?

Prayer

God, the source of possibility, open our eyes to see opportunities to give, that the lives of others may be enhanced and our faith renewed, through the example of Jesus Christ our Lord. *Amen.*

Mark 13:1-13

13 As he came out of the temple, one of his disciples said to him, "Look, Teacher, what large stones and what large buildings!" ²Then Jesus asked him, "Do you see these great buildings? Not one stone will be left here upon another; all will be thrown down."

³When he was sitting on the Mount of Olives opposite the temple, Peter, James, John, and Andrew asked him privately, ⁴"Tell us, when will this be, and what will be the sign that all these things are about to be accomplished?" ⁵Then Jesus began to say to them, "Beware that no one leads you astray. ⁶Many will come in my name and say, 'I am he!' and they will lead many astray. ⁷When you hear of wars and rumors of wars, do not be alarmed; this must take place, but the end is still to come. ⁸For nation will rise against nation, and kingdom against kingdom; there will be earthquakes in various places; there will be famines. This is but the beginning of the birthpangs.

⁹"As for yourselves, beware; for they will hand you over to councils; and you will be beaten in synagogues; and you will stand before governors and kings because of me, as a testimony to them. ¹⁰And the good news must first be proclaimed to all nations. ¹¹When they bring you to trial and hand you over, do not worry beforehand about what you are to say; but say whatever is given you at that time, for it is not you who speak, but the Holy Spirit. ¹²Brother will betray brother to death, and a father his child, and children will rise against parents and have them put to death; ¹³and you will be hated by all because of my name. But the one who endures to the end will be saved.

Reflection

Is faith meant to calm fear? Many people certainly hope so. Instability of all sorts seemingly prevails around the world, and with instability, tremendous fear surfaces. The search for something reliable intensifies. Much has proven unreliable; for many, only Jesus is the answer. This passage gives no reassurance. Jesus declares that the temple at Jerusalem will fall, and it does. Jesus also resists the pleas of his disciples. They want signs that will alert them to the onset of tribulation. Instead he warns them not to be led astray.

Worse, he foresees a time of conflict when even families will be divided. His followers will be persecuted for their faith, as indeed happens and continues today. Meanwhile there will be natural disasters as well as social unrest. The future looks bleak.

In this passage, as in various gospel accounts, the core issue is faith. What are the qualities of faith? The disciples' questions reveal their intense search. On what can they rely? All that seems sacred will crumble. What will be left?

Jesus notes, "The good news must first be proclaimed to all nations." He adds, "The one who endures to the end will be saved." Though he does not elaborate, clearly faith requires focus on core purpose. Amid threats, Jesus' followers must not lose this focus.

Further, amid upheaval, good news is needed. This is paradoxical and elusive in the passage. But focus and endurance in the midst of trial are key qualities of faith.

The Rev. William L. Sachs, PhD.
Director of the Center for Interfaith Reconciliation,
St. Stephen's Church
Richmond, Virginia

Questions

How does faith in Jesus Christ serve us in times of fear?

What does it mean to be led astray?

At what points in your life have you been led astray?

Prayer

God of hope, give us, in the midst of our trials, a sense of your purpose and a readiness to follow, that your good news may be proclaimed, through Christ our Lord. *Amen.*

Mark 13:14-27

[14]"But when you see the desolating sacrilege set up where it ought not to be (let the reader understand), then those in Judea must flee to the mountains; [15]the one on the housetop must not go down or enter the house to take anything away; [16]the one in the field must not turn back to get a coat. [17]Woe to those who are pregnant and to those who are nursing infants in those days! [18]Pray that it may not be in winter. [19]For in those days there will be suffering, such as has not been from the beginning of the creation that God created until now, no, and never will be. [20]And if the Lord had not cut short those days, no one would be saved; but for the sake of the elect, whom he chose, he has cut short those days. [21]And if anyone says to you at that time, 'Look! Here is the Messiah!' or 'Look! There he is!' —do not believe it. [22]False messiahs and false prophets will appear and produce signs and omens, to lead astray, if possible, the elect. [23]But be alert; I have already told you everything.

[24]"But in those days, after that suffering, the sun will be darkened, and the moon will not give its light, [25]and the stars will be falling from heaven, and the powers in the heavens will be shaken.

[26]Then they will see 'the Son of Man coming in clouds' with great power and glory. [27]Then he will send out the angels, and gather his elect from the four winds, from the ends of the earth to the ends of heaven.

Reflection

What is the worst thing you can imagine? In Jewish history it was "the desolating sacrilege," a phrase which occurs three times in Daniel (9:27, 11:31, 12:11) and in 1 Maccabees, where it describes God's temple being taken over, defiled, and polluted in 168 BCE by the pagan king Antiochus.

Jesus uses this phrase from a past event to speak about the future—it points to a type of event rather than a particular event. When you face a devastating horror, don't be deceived by people claiming that this is "the end." Moments of horrendous evil will come. As "labor pains" they demonstrate that new creation is needed and is coming, but a painful contraction in labor doesn't prove that birth is imminent. We must endure but can take comfort that God is at work lessening the evil ("cutting short" those days).

"The sun will be darkened" or "the stars will be falling from heaven," are phrases used in the Old Testament to describe earth-shattering events, which do not leave the earth literally shattered (e.g. Isaiah 13:6-10). The Son of Man refers to Daniel 7:13-14, where God's people suffer but God vindicates them. Jesus uses this phrase to describe his death and resurrection (e.g. Mark 14:62). In the end, God decisively ends his people's suffering and vindicates them.

Thus when we face great suffering, it doesn't prove that God doesn't care, or that the end has come. No. We must endure, knowing that God is active even in terrible times, and that God will eventually bring justice.

The Rev. Jeremy Duff
Vicar of St. Paul's Church
Widnes, England

Questions

What has been the worst time in your life? Can you see any sign that God was alongside you during it? *my miscarriages*

Jesus suffered before being rescued and vindicated. Are you prepared to face the same journey? *I felt my heavenly Father very near as I sobbed, John was so tender – he assured me we'd have children! How blessed we have been!*

Prayer

Father God, we pray for those who face terrible suffering today. Lessen their pain, give them the strength and courage to endure, and act in power to bring their suffering to an end. We ask this in the name of Jesus who suffered, died, and rose again for us. *Amen.*

Mark 13:28-37

28"From the fig tree learn its lesson: as soon as its branch becomes tender and puts forth its leaves, you know that summer is near. 29So also, when you see these things taking place, you know that he is near, at the very gates. 30Truly I tell you, this generation will not pass away until all these things have taken place. 31Heaven and earth will pass away, but my words will not pass away.

32"But about that day or hour no one knows, neither the angels in heaven, nor the Son, but only the Father. 33Beware, keep alert; for you do not know when the time will come. 34It is like a man going on a journey, when he leaves home and puts his slaves in charge, each with his work, and commands the doorkeeper to be on the watch. 35Therefore, keep awake—for you do not know when the master of the house will come, in the evening, or at midnight, or at cockcrow, or at dawn, 36or else he may find you asleep when he comes suddenly. 37And what I say to you I say to all: Keep awake."

Reflection

We return to the question that began this chapter of the gospel. When? What will be the signs? Overall, Jesus' answer has been clear: nobody knows. There will be no signs; just stay alert. But how does this fit with the parable of the fig tree?

The tree's leaves are not a very precise indicator of time. They tell you summer is coming, but not that summer will be here in 13,497 minutes. It is like a painful contraction that tells you the baby is coming but not whether you need endure another five minutes or five hours. We learn from the fig tree that "near" is as near as we are going to get. This brings with it two dangers: We might be deceived by people saying "it's here" when it's not, and we might "fall asleep," acting as if it will never happen.

What are "all these things" that will happen before this generation passes away? This statement is roughly equivalent to verse 9:1: "There are some standing here who will not taste death until they see that the kingdom of God has come with power." God's kingdom would come in power in their lifetime. The Son of Man would receive power and glory from God. God would act decisively to save his people. God did this by raising Jesus from the dead, and through this, death itself was defeated, opening a new and living way for all people to have peace with God and receive God's Spirit. That has happened. We are in "the last days" (Acts 2:17). He is near. Keep awake.

The Rev. Jeremy Duff
Vicar of St. Paul's Church
Widnes, England

Questions

What difference does it make that Jesus will return, and that he might do so tomorrow?

What does it mean for you to keep awake today?

Prayer

Lord Jesus, you know it is hard for us to truly believe that you will return soon, and yet not get caught up in foolish speculation. Give us patience and urgency in right measure as we live for you today. *Amen.*

Mark 14:1-11

14 It was two days before the Passover and the festival of Unleavened Bread. The chief priests and the scribes were looking for a way to arrest Jesus by stealth and kill him; ²for they said, "Not during the festival, or there may be a riot among the people."

³While he was at Bethany in the house of Simon the leper, as he sat at the table, a woman came with an alabaster jar of very costly ointment of nard, and she broke open the jar and poured the ointment on his head. ⁴But some were there who said to one another in anger, "Why was the ointment wasted in this way? ⁵For this ointment could have been sold for more than three hundred denarii, and the money given to the poor." And they scolded her. ⁶But Jesus said, "Let her alone; why do you trouble her? She has performed a good service for me. ⁷For you always have the poor with you, and you can show kindness to them whenever you wish; but you will not always have me. ⁸She has done what she could; she has anointed my body beforehand for its burial. ⁹Truly I tell you, wherever the good news is proclaimed in the whole world, what she has done will be told in remembrance of her."

¹⁰Then Judas Iscariot, who was one of the twelve, went to the chief priests in order to betray him to them. ¹¹When they heard it, they were greatly pleased, and promised to give him money. So he began to look for an opportunity to betray him.

Reflection

Both *The Wall Street Journal* and *The New York Times* regularly feature series of obituaries. Although they write about accomplished souls who are relatively unknown to the average citizen, these remarkable lives almost always contain an aspect of the deceased's life that is a memorable surprise.

That unusual twist is always some special gift or contribution that intrigues the obituary reader to ponder more seriously the unique value of this previously unfamiliar person. What we tend to remember about each other are those quirky stories, those out-of-character moments where the common is overshadowed by the profound.

When the woman broke the jar of pure nard over Jesus' head, the common moment suddenly became extraordinary. The same thing happens when you and I extend ourselves beyond the polite moment by pouring a unique word of love or affection on another.

Unlike this biblical woman, we tend to hold back, hesitate, and resist the very urge to move beyond our comfort zones of expressed affection. When we do extend ourselves, it will be remembered as was the nard. Maybe even in our obituary.

The Rev. Dr. Daniel P. Matthews
Rector Emeritus, Trinity Church Wall Street
New York, New York

Question

What is it within me that hinders and stifles my risking an overt expression of fondness and affection? I'm so grateful God made me a friendly person. I like to chat with "strangers" They are not strange - just normal people. I often give them a compliment it makes me feel good when they smile & thank me!

Prayer

Lord, help me to love with abandon and express those deep feelings of closeness and affection I yearn to share. *Amen.*

Mark 14:12-25

[12]On the first day of Unleavened Bread, when the Passover lamb is sacrificed, his disciples said to him, "Where do you want us to go and make the preparations for you to eat the Passover?" [13]So he sent two of his disciples, saying to them, "Go into the city, and a man carrying a jar of water will meet you; follow him, [14]and wherever he enters, say to the owner of the house, 'The Teacher asks, Where is my guest room where I may eat the Passover with my disciples?' [15]He will show you a large room upstairs, furnished and ready. Make preparations for us there." [16]So the disciples set out and went to the city, and found everything as he had told them; and they prepared the Passover meal.

[17]When it was evening, he came with the twelve. [18]And when they had taken their places and were eating, Jesus said, "Truly I tell you, one of you will betray me, one who is eating with me." [19]They began to be distressed and to say to him one after another, "Surely, not I?" [20]He said to them, "It is one of the twelve, one who is dipping bread into the bowl with me. [21]For the Son of Man goes as it is written of him, but woe to that one by whom the Son of Man is betrayed! It would have been better for that one not to have been born."

[22]While they were eating, he took a loaf of bread, and after blessing it he broke it, gave it to them, and said, "Take; this is my body." [23]Then he took a cup, and after giving thanks he gave it to them, and all of them drank from it. [24]He said to them, "This is my blood of

the covenant, which is poured out for many. [25]Truly I tell you, I will never again drink of the fruit of the vine until that day when I drink it new in the kingdom of God."

Reflection

The dominant culture holds the solitary individual in great esteem. Personal rights and privileges are thought of as the very bedrock of our western culture.

In Philadelphia a relatively new museum commemorates the United States Constitution and its intriguing formulation. As the museum visitor enters the darkened introductory space, an actor appears in a spotlighted circle beneath the visitors' circular seats. After a period of silence, the pause is broken with a booming stage voice, "We the People."

The entire museum reiterates those three words in ways that clearly challenge our dominant culture's emphasis on "me" and "I." The "we" makes the Constitution such a profound document, created by that astounding group in the summer of 1787.

At the Last Supper, Jesus held a common cup shared by each disciple. It was the ultimate "we" gesture. I am my brother's keeper despite the noise of our dominant culture to the contrary. When we break the bread and share the common cup, we remember and make present that first Eucharist and the daily challenge to be at one with our neighbor.

The Rev. Dr. Daniel P. Matthews
Rector Emeritus, Trinity Church Wall Street
New York, New York

Questions

Have you ever thought how unusual it is that we share a common cup at a public Lord's Supper? What might this say about our understanding of "we" as part of our faith?

Prayer

Help me, O Lord, amidst my world of winner-take-all, to hold fast the biblical truth that I am in fact my brother's keeper. *Amen.*

Mark 14:26-42

[26]When they had sung the hymn, they went out to the Mount of Olives. [27]And Jesus said to them, "You will all become deserters; for it is written, 'I will strike the shepherd, and the sheep will be scattered.'

[28]But after I am raised up, I will go before you to Galilee." [29]Peter said to him, "Even though all become deserters, I will not." [30]Jesus said to him, "Truly I tell you, this day, this very night, before the cock crows twice, you will deny me three times." [31]But he said vehemently, "Even though I must die with you, I will not deny you." And all of them said the same.

[32]They went to a place called Gethsemane; and he said to his disciples, "Sit here while I pray." [33]He took with him Peter and James and John, and began to be distressed and agitated. [34]And he said to them, "I am deeply grieved, even to death; remain here, and keep awake." [35]And going a little farther, he threw himself on the ground and prayed that, if it were possible, the hour might pass from him. [36]He said, "Abba, Father, for you all things are possible; remove this cup from me; yet, not what I want, but what you want." [37]He came and found them sleeping; and he said to Peter, "Simon, are you asleep? Could you not keep awake one hour? [38]Keep awake and pray that you may not come into the time of trial; the spirit indeed is willing, but the flesh is weak." [39]And again he went away and prayed, saying the same words. [40]And once more he came and found them sleeping, for their eyes were very heavy; and they did not know what to say to him. [41]He came a third time

and said to them, "Are you still sleeping and taking your rest? Enough! The hour has come; the Son of Man is betrayed into the hands of sinners. [42]Get up, let us be going. See, my betrayer is at hand."

Reflection

It seems a bit tough on Peter that his betrayal of Jesus had to be foretold. It makes him look doubly awful, because it implies that Peter was forewarned and so should have been forearmed. But Peter does not know himself. He is living, as so many of us do, with a fantasy self. Peter's fantasy self tells him that he will never desert Jesus, and Jesus will be so grateful when Peter, alone of all the disciples, sticks with Jesus and saves him.

And yet, while this fantasy self is busy doing Jesus' job for him and saving the world, the real Peter sleeps as Jesus faces his coming death. Jesus' fate is as much foretold as Peter's betrayal. But Jesus knows himself. He knows his fear and his longing to find another way to fulfill his calling. He also knows that the very core of his being is obedience to the Father.

Peter might have said, before the cock crowed three times, that his whole being was defined by his loyalty to Jesus; he was a disciple through and through. He discovers otherwise. And that is one of the indications we have that Jesus is truly the Son of the Father: Nothing, however horrific, however full of natural human fear, will make Jesus change his essential character, the one defined by the Father. His "godhead" is not defined by his power, but by the fact that he is the Son of the Father, always.

Jane Williams
Theologian and Author
London, England

Questions

Can you think of parts of yourself that might be, like Peter's, a "fantasy self?"

What do you think is the most essential definition of who you are? Could anything make you betray that? How could you prevent that from happening?

Prayer

God of grace, you know us better than we know ourselves: Draw us by your compassionate and truthful gaze into a true knowledge of ourselves, and lead us forward to the place where you can trust us, like Peter, with the message of your good news. *Amen.*

Mark 14:43-65

⁴³Immediately, while he was still speaking, Judas, one of the twelve, arrived; and with him there was a crowd with swords and clubs, from the chief priests, the scribes, and the elders. ⁴⁴Now the betrayer had given them a sign, saying, "The one I will kiss is the man; arrest him and lead him away under guard." ⁴⁵So when he came, he went up to him at once and said, "Rabbi!" and kissed him. ⁴⁶Then they laid hands on him and arrested him. ⁴⁷But one of those who stood near drew his sword and struck the slave of the high priest, cutting off his ear. ⁴⁸Then Jesus said to them, "Have you come out with swords and clubs to arrest me as though I were a bandit? ⁴⁹Day after day I was with you in the temple teaching, and you did not arrest me. But let the scriptures be fulfilled." ⁵⁰All of them deserted him and fled.

⁵¹A certain young man was following him, wearing nothing but a linen cloth. They caught hold of him, ⁵²but he left the linen cloth and ran off naked.

⁵³They took Jesus to the high priest; and all the chief priests, the elders, and the scribes were assembled. ⁵⁴Peter had followed him at a distance, right into the courtyard of the high priest; and he was sitting with the guards, warming himself at the fire. ⁵⁵Now the chief priests and the whole council were looking for testimony against Jesus to put him to death; but they found none. ⁵⁶For many gave false testimony against him, and their testimony did not agree. ⁵⁷Some stood up and gave false testimony against him, saying,

58"We heard him say, 'I will destroy this temple that is made with hands, and in three days I will build another, not made with hands.'" 59But even on this point their testimony did not agree. 60Then the high priest stood up before them and asked Jesus, "Have you no answer? What is it that they testify against you?" 61But he was silent and did not answer. Again the high priest asked him, "Are you the Messiah, the Son of the Blessed One?" 62Jesus said, "I am; and 'you will see the Son of Man seated at the right hand of the Power,' and 'coming with the clouds of heaven.'"

63Then the high priest tore his clothes and said, "Why do we still need witnesses? 64You have heard his blasphemy! What is your decision?" All of them condemned him as deserving death. 65Some began to spit on him, to blindfold him, and to strike him, saying to him, "Prophesy!" The guards also took him over and beat him.

Reflection

The very name Judas has become a byword for treachery. We all like a good scapegoat. The truth of the matter is that all of Jesus' disciples betrayed him. They ran away, they hid behind closed doors, they denied that they had anything do with him. The unnamed young man who would rather run naked through the streets than stand by Jesus is a symbol of all of Jesus' disciples, then and now.

Admittedly, Judas led the mob to Jesus and helped them identify their man in the scrum and the dim light. But Jesus himself says that they could have found him any time. He was hardly in hiding. One day soon, with or without Judas, Jesus would have ended up on the cross. They were clearly ready for him, with their kangaroo court and their false witnesses; Judas was just a bonus, an added turn of the screw. Look Jesus, even your own disciples doubt you.

The eucharistic prayer of confession says that we have failed God and each other by what we have done and by what we have left undone; both are failures. So Jesus stands alone and faces his accusers, because we have failed him by what we have done and by what we have left undone. Not one of us is innocent. Not one of us is outside the invitation to forgiveness. All of us have betrayed him. Call us Judas, call us Peter, call us a young man running through the streets in naked fear.

Jane Williams
Theologian and Author
London, England

Questions

What is the thing you are most ashamed of in your whole life?

Have you received God's forgiveness for that? If so, how? If not, what might enable you to receive that forgiveness?

Prayer

God of all, we have betrayed you endlessly, through fear, ignorance, and selfishness. Forgive us, and strengthen us in the knowledge of your forgiving love, so that betrayal of you and of each other becomes more and more alien to us, as we grow in the likeness of Christ. *Amen.*

A Journey with Mark

Mark 14:66-72

⁶⁶While Peter was below in the courtyard, one of the servant-girls of the high priest came by. ⁶⁷When she saw Peter warming himself, she stared at him and said, "You also were with Jesus, the man from Nazareth." ⁶⁸But he denied it, saying, "I do not know or understand what you are talking about." And he went out into the forecourt. Then the cock crowed. ⁶⁹And the servant-girl, on seeing him, began again to say to the bystanders, "This man is one of them." ⁷⁰But again he denied it. Then after a little while the bystanders again said to Peter, "Certainly you are one of them; for you are a Galilean." ⁷¹But he began to curse, and he swore an oath, "I do not know this man you are talking about." ⁷²At that moment the cock crowed for the second time. Then Peter remembered that Jesus had said to him, "Before the cock crows twice, you will deny me three times." And he broke down and wept.

Reflection

Fear has a dramatic impact on human behavior. In this very human story, we see the apostle Peter spiral into apostasy and denial of his Lord. It is awful to consider how quickly this happens for someone who has shared so much with Jesus. Whether through grief, guilt, or just panic, Peter ends in tears. He is at the end of his own reserves and is confronted by the fact of what he has just said and done.

The enduring fact for us is that through our baptism into Christ we are marked as Christ's own forever. From our perspective of the biblical narrative, we know how Peter is restored from this place of fear and humiliation by the Lord so that he could truly be the rock of faith that Jesus wanted him to be. Of course few Christians intend, either at a personal or corporate level, to fail Jesus in a testing time. The consequences are so awful that we need to do all we can to guard against it. If we relied only on the reserves of our human frailty, we could not hope to endure. Ultimately Peter had to rely fully on God's grace. He needed to approach Jesus with the confidence that it was Jesus rather than Peter himself who was the fully reliable one.

The Most Rev. Dr. Philip Freier
Archbishop of Melbourne and Primate of Australia
Melbourne, Australia

A Journey with Mark

Question

Hebrews 4:16 exhorts us "to approach the throne of grace with boldness, so that we may receive mercy and find grace to help in time of need." How confident are you in approaching our Lord Jesus in times of failure and disappointment?

Prayer

Lord Jesus Christ, you reach out to us in all of our human need. Increase our trust in you so that we may always know you are a friend and advocate in our time of need. Forgive us our failures and grant us confidence to always come to you in prayer. *Amen.*

Mark 15:1-15

15 As soon as it was morning, the chief priests held a consultation with the elders and scribes and the whole council. They bound Jesus, led him away, and handed him over to Pilate. ²Pilate asked him, "Are you the King of the Jews?" He answered him, "You say so." ³Then the chief priests accused him of many things. ⁴Pilate asked him again, "Have you no answer? See how many charges they bring against you." ⁵But Jesus made no further reply, so that Pilate was amazed.

⁶Now at the festival he used to release a prisoner for them, anyone for whom they asked. ⁷Now a man called Barabbas was in prison with the rebels who had committed murder during the insurrection. ⁸So the crowd came and began to ask Pilate to do for them according to his custom. ⁹Then he answered them, "Do you want me to release for you the King of the Jews?" ¹⁰For he realized that it was out of jealousy that the chief priests had handed him over. ¹¹But the chief priests stirred up the crowd to have him release Barabbas for them instead. ¹²Pilate spoke to them again, "Then what do you wish me to do with the man you call the King of the Jews?" ¹³They shouted back, "Crucify him!" ¹⁴Pilate asked them, "Why, what evil has he done?" But they shouted all the more, "Crucify him!" ¹⁵So Pilate, wishing to satisfy the crowd, released Barabbas for them; and after flogging Jesus, he handed him over to be crucified.

Reflection

One of our foundational problems is that we readily imagine that we have control over God. This principle was at work in the thinking of the crowd that gathered before Pilate. Pilate had the power to release a prisoner, and the crowd had the power to influence Pilate's decision. The choice was clear: Jesus, whom they had known as a worker of the many signs of the kingdom, or Barabbas, the rebel and murderer.

This was their choice, and it was not as stark as it might seem. Both men were in their own way a threat to the Roman order, which the people of Jerusalem resented but knew they were powerless to resist. Barabbas was an insurrectionist, hostile to the Roman occupation of Jerusalem. For a repressed people, the annual opportunity to be allowed to gather and put forth a position that Pilate would implement must have been greatly anticipated. They quickly came with one voice to call for the release of Barabbas. A put-down for Pilate and the Romans, it seemed a decision that resulted in a boost of confidence for the crowd.

Whatever motivations were at work, the voice of the crowd led to the condemnation of Jesus. Two men stood before them—one released and one sentenced to death. The crowd and all who have denied Jesus since that day resolve the question through human thinking, which is far from recognition of the divine plan that remains at work in Jesus.

The Most Rev. Dr. Philip Freier
Archbishop of Melbourne and Primate of Australia
Melbourne, Australia

Question

Can you recall a time where you have preferred the satisfaction of your human desires over those things that God has intended for you through Jesus?

Prayer

Loving Father, we approach the cross of Jesus with reverence. We know too well our ability to please ourselves, and not to please you. Thank you for the faithfulness of your son, our Lord Jesus Christ, who gave himself into human hands and death for our salvation. *Amen.*

Mark 15:16-32

¹⁶Then the soldiers led him into the courtyard of the palace (that is, the governor's headquarters); and they called together the whole cohort. ¹⁷And they clothed him in a purple cloak; and after twisting some thorns into a crown, they put it on him. ¹⁸And they began saluting him, "Hail, King of the Jews!" ¹⁹They struck his head with a reed, spat upon him, and knelt down in homage to him. ²⁰After mocking him, they stripped him of the purple cloak and put his own clothes on him. Then they led him out to crucify him.

²¹They compelled a passer-by, who was coming in from the country, to carry his cross; it was Simon of Cyrene, the father of Alexander and Rufus. ²²Then they brought Jesus to the place called Golgotha (which means the place of a skull). ²³And they offered him wine mixed with myrrh; but he did not take it. ²⁴And they crucified him, and divided his clothes among them, casting lots to decide what each should take.

²⁵It was nine o'clock in the morning when they crucified him. ²⁶The inscription of the charge against him read, "The King of the Jews." ²⁷And with him they crucified two bandits, one on his right and one on his left. ²⁹Those who passed by derided him, shaking their heads and saying, "Aha! You who would destroy the temple and build it in three days, ³⁰save yourself, and come down from the cross!" ³¹In the same way the chief priests, along with the scribes, were also mocking him among themselves and saying, "He saved others; he cannot save himself. ³²Let the Messiah, the

King of Israel, come down from the cross now, so that we may see and believe." Those who were crucified with him also taunted him.

Reflection

Can we know a person by the company they keep? Mark thought so. The company Jesus kept is Mark's way of indicating to us what sort of man the Son of Man is.

Note the soldiers. The authorities had to quash what Jesus stood for; naturally they used the shock troops of violent oppression. Kingship—public leadership of God's people—was the best way to sum up the charge against Jesus. Crucifixion was reserved for Roman traitors. Note Simon, a rural worker, probably Gentile, who alone accompanies Jesus in stark contrast both with the condemning urban elites and with the fickle peasant crowd last seen thronging the path in 11:8.

See the two robbers. They are not petty thieves but organized bandits who upset the peace of Rome to the delight of the oppressed populace. Jesus never follows their patriotic, violent ways, and he is in turn mocked by them. But it is to them, and not to the misguided disciples that falls the honor of being on Jesus' right and left.

Jesus acted, and was seen to act, as a public figure leading a public movement with public consequences. His was not a private ministry calling people to an individualistic inner religion but an open call for people to affiliate with the new thing that he was doing. It was a new thing that offered immediate (and long-term) social and political upheaval, not least for groups driven by nationalistic ethnic privilege and imperial pretentions to power.

Dr. Stephen Backhouse
Lecturer in Social and Political Theology,
St. Mellitus College
London, England

Questions

How does the phrase "Jesus is Lord" make you feel? *safe* Does this differ from what someone living in first-century, Roman-occupied Palestine would have felt? What is the difference?

I'm not sure — I guess they felt very un safe — Threatened & fearful.

Prayer

Jesus, you said follow me, be born again, and the kingdom of God is here. You are doing something new. As we form our company around you, we welcome your presence among us. Come, Lord Jesus. *Amen.*

A Journey with Mark

Mark 15:33-47

[33]When it was noon, darkness came over the whole land until three in the afternoon. [34]At three o'clock Jesus cried out with a loud voice, "Eloi, Eloi, lema sabachthani?" which means, "My God, my God, why have you forsaken me?" [35]When some of the bystanders heard it, they said, "Listen, he is calling for Elijah." [36]And someone ran, filled a sponge with sour wine, put it on a stick, and gave it to him to drink, saying, "Wait, let us see whether Elijah will come to take him down." [37]Then Jesus gave a loud cry and breathed his last. [38]And the curtain of the temple was torn in two, from top to bottom. [39]Now when the centurion, who stood facing him, saw that in this way he breathed his last, he said, "Truly this man was God's Son!"

[40]There were also women looking on from a distance; among them were Mary Magdalene, and Mary the mother of James the younger and of Joses, and Salome. [41]These used to follow him and provided for him when he was in Galilee; and there were many other women who had come up with him to Jerusalem.

[42]When evening had come, and since it was the day of Preparation, that is, the day before the sabbath, [43]Joseph of Arimathea, a respected member of the council, who was also himself waiting expectantly for the kingdom of God, went boldly to Pilate and asked for the body of Jesus. [44]Then Pilate wondered if he were already dead; and summoning the centurion, he asked him whether he had been dead for some time. [45]When he learned from the centurion that he was dead, he granted the body to Joseph. [46]Then Joseph

bought a linen cloth, and taking down the body, wrapped it in the linen cloth, and laid it in a tomb that had been hewn out of the rock. He then rolled a stone against the door of the tomb. [47]Mary Magdalene and Mary the mother of Joses saw where the body was laid.

Reflection

The earliest followers of Jesus encapsulate his life with one word: *euangelion*—gospel. It is a military term, calling to mind the welcome news of a victorious siege. King Jesus is the one who has rescued us from the present evil age (Galatians 1:4).

For Mark, two main forces of the evil age come to a head at the crucifixion: temple and empire.

The temple represents more than merely religion. It is the repository of the hopes and fears of God's chosen people. It is synonymous with the privilege of living under God's law. It is the primary symbol for ethnic purity, the sign of a people set apart and awaiting national and racial vindication. At the cross, the torn temple curtain is a tearing down of a whole set of assumptions about what it is to live as a chosen people under God's rule.

Another power is present at the cross. Crucifixion was for enemies of the Roman Empire. The centurion is not a symbol of heroic courage. He is the hated enemy. The pretensions of overweening, imperial power are met in him. The soldier did not invent the title Son of God: it was stamped onto every coin in his pocket as a proclamation of Caesar. To gain this position required grasping and pride. To retain it required violence and guile. And yet, at the cross of a broken traitor, the confession is wrested from the oppressor. Surely this man was the son of God.

Dr. Stephen Backhouse
Lecturer in Social and Political Theology,
St. Mellitus College
London, England

Questions

How do the forces of pride, purity, privilege, and power manifest themselves today?

In what ways might a cruciform life offer welcome news to our present evil age?

Prayer

Lord Jesus, you have told us to take up our cross and follow you. Give us what we need to obey you in this present age. With the first people who recognized your saving presence, we pray Hosanna. Save us King Jesus! *Amen.*

Mark 16:1-8

16 When the sabbath was over, Mary Magdalene, and Mary the mother of James, and Salome bought spices, so that they might go and anoint him. ²And very early on the first day of the week, when the sun had risen, they went to the tomb. ³They had been saying to one another, "Who will roll away the stone for us from the entrance to the tomb?" ⁴When they looked up, they saw that the stone, which was very large, had already been rolled back. ⁵As they entered the tomb, they saw a young man, dressed in a white robe, sitting on the right side; and they were alarmed. ⁶But he said to them, "Do not be alarmed; you are looking for Jesus of Nazareth, who was crucified. He has been raised; he is not here. Look, there is the place they laid him. ⁷But go, tell his disciples and Peter that he is going ahead of you to Galilee; there you will see him, just as he told you." ⁸So they went out and fled from the tomb, for terror and amazement had seized them; and they said nothing to anyone, for they were afraid.

Reflection

The extraordinary events of the first Easter morning are the heart of our faith as Christians. Here our baptism becomes literally a matter of death and life, for we are baptized into the death of Jesus that we may walk with him in the newness of his risen life (Romans 6:4).

There is no matter-of-fact way of describing this—it is a meeting of fact and faith. So Mark invites us to dare to believe by describing where Jesus is not. He introduces the young man who tells the faithful women what has happened.

Many people reflect on the empty tomb. I think more often about the stone rolled away. The stone rolled up symbolizes the end of hope. It affirms the incontrovertible permanence of the death of Jesus. The stone rolled away throws open the tomb for the working of God's amazing resurrection power.

The women come in their faithfulness to honor and anoint Jesus' body. Like people everywhere who come to carry out works of grace, they worry about the practical details. Who will roll away the stone?

But they find that God's power has been there before them. They find the young man who tells them that they will see Jesus just as he told them. No wonder the women go away in terror and amazement. God has broken through to the world in a new reality. In the end there is no alternative: they must go and tell.

The Most Rev. David Chillingworth
Bishop of St. Andrews, Dunkeld and Dunblane
Primus of the Scottish Episcopal Church
Perth, Scotland

A Journey with Mark

Question

We too are called to "go and tell." When you tell the good news of the Resurrection of Jesus and what it means for you, what do you say?

I wear the cross John gave me for my 50th and try to smile at people and chat with strangers and hand out "Peace Pilgrim" bklets and with each one I pray it will lead them to Christ. I say to my JP customers spiritual health is far more important than physical

Prayer

Lord,

So many stones are rolled up at the door of our hopes.

Give us new faith in your power

To roll away stones

To empty tombs

And to triumph over sin and death.

Amen.

Mark 16:9-20

⁹Now after he rose early on the first day of the week, he appeared first to Mary Magdalene, from whom he had cast out seven demons. ¹⁰She went out and told those who had been with him, while they were mourning and weeping. ¹¹But when they heard that he was alive and had been seen by her, they would not believe it.

¹²After this he appeared in another form to two of them, as they were walking into the country. ¹³And they went back and told the rest, but they did not believe them.

¹⁴Later he appeared to the eleven themselves as they were sitting at the table; and he upbraided them for their lack of faith and stubbornness, because they had not believed those who saw him after he had risen. ¹⁵And he said to them, "Go into all the world and proclaim the good news to the whole creation. ¹⁶The one who believes and is baptized will be saved; but the one who does not believe will be condemned. ¹⁷And these signs will accompany those who believe: by using my name they will cast out demons; they will speak in new tongues; ¹⁸they will pick up snakes in their hands, and if they drink any deadly thing, it will not hurt them; they will lay their hands on the sick, and they will recover."

¹⁹So then the Lord Jesus, after he had spoken to them, was taken up into heaven and sat down at the right hand of God. ²⁰And they went out and proclaimed the good news everywhere, while the Lord worked with them and confirmed the message by the signs that accompanied it.

Reflection

Would you have believed if they told you that Jesus was alive? The disciples had a poor track record. The people whom Jesus healed and helped ignored his pleas that they should tell no one.

I have conducted hundreds of funerals in my time. Standing in front of the coffins of dearly loved members of my congregation, I have declared—and sometimes shouted defiantly—the good news of resurrection hope. And as I've shouted it and sometimes whispered it, I've asked myself whether I believe. I want to know if it is true for me also.

And that's a challenge. Much of the main business at a funeral is about comforting the bereaved—about recognizing and accepting the reality of death—while standing by an open grave and reflecting on the final reality of our days on earth.

I firmly believe that there is a dogged resurrection belief in many people. It enables them to face both life and death calm and unafraid. It is expressed in turns of phrase like, "We'll meet again one day." But somehow it isn't yet a joyful reality.

So the disciples struggled when Mary Magdalene and the other disciples came and told what had happened. Jesus had foretold it. They had heard him say it over and over again. But believing it as a practical reality was beyond them.

And we ourselves are often confused and uncertain, wanting to believe and yet not quite sure.

The telling and retelling of this huge truth has been the seed bed from which the universal church has sprung. And we are part of that—telling and retelling so that gradually it becomes the very center of life and faith.

The Most Rev. David Chillingworth
Bishop of St. Andrews, Dunkeld and Dunblane
Primus of the Scottish Episcopal Church
Perth, Scotland

A Journey with Mark

Questions

Death is inevitable and unavoidable. Does faith in Christ's Resurrection change the way you think about your own death? *Yes*

How? *I do believe that God who created the universes could and did bring His Son back to life – easy for Him. I also believe vs 16. I want to believe the unbelievers meet Jesus and accept Him in the last seconds so none of His loved ones go to Hell for His love is so huge He loves each person He created!*

Prayer

Lord, increase our faith.

Like the disciples, we find it hard to believe

That you are alive and present with us for ever.

Give us the eyes of faith to see you and to know you.

Go with us as we tell others of your power over sin and death.

Amen.

About the Authors

W. Frank Allen has served as rector of St. David's (Radnor) Church in Wayne, Pennsylvania, since 1997. This is a church on a mission to know God in Jesus Christ and make Christ known to others. He is married to Amy, and they have three grown sons. Frank writes a weekly blog on God's working in our lives that can be followed on St. David's website, http://www.stdavidschurch.org/.

Stephen Backhouse is a lecturer in social and political theology at St. Mellitus College in London, England.

David Chillingworth is bishop of St. Andrews, Dunkeld and Dunblane, and primus of the Scottish Episcopal Church. Before moving to Scotland in 2005, Bishop David served in the Church of Ireland in Northern Ireland. He believes that his vocation to a ministry of reconciliation changed to a vocation in missional leadership.

C. Andrew Doyle is the bishop of the Episcopal Diocese of Texas and author of *Unabashedly Episcopalian*. He enjoys conversations about the future of the Church mission.

Jeremy Duff is the vicar of St. Paul's Church in Widnes, England. Alongside his passion for church growth, he has an established writing and teaching ministry, including posts at Liverpool Cathedral, Oxford University, and St. Mellitus College, London. His latest book on Mark's Gospel is *Peter's Preaching*.

Philip Freir is the archbishop of Melbourne and the primate of Australia. Before coming to Melbourne in 2006, he was bishop of the Northern Territory and had previously served in parishes in Queensland, including in remote Aboriginal and Torres Strait

Islander communities. He is strongly committed to issues of reconciliation, to developing rural ministry, to ministry and mission in the Asian Century, and to a renewed vision for Australia.

Deirdre Good is professor of New Testament at The General Theological Seminary in New York City. She specializes in the synoptic gospels, Christian origins, non-canonical writings and biblical languages. She grew up in Kenya, where her parents were missionaries. She is a frequent contributor to the blog *Episcopal Café.*

Margaret Guenther is an Episcopal priest and professor emerita of The General Theological Seminary in New York City. She is also the author of several books, including *Holy Listening: The Art of Spiritual Direction; Toward Holy Ground; The Practice of Prayer;* and *Notes from a Sojourner Walking Home: From Eden to Emmaus.*

Fred Hiltz is the primate of the Anglican Church of Canada and is formerly bishop of Nova Scotia and Prince Edward Island. He was elected as thirteenth primate of the Anglican Church of Canada in June 2007. He leads the Church in discerning and pursuing the mission of God.

Brenda G. Husson has served as the rector of St. James' Church in New York City since 1996. A large, urban parish known for its vibrant worship and a deeply rooted ministry with children and families, the parish during her tenure has extended its ministries of service and its opportunities for Bible study for all ages. Her particular passions in ministry are Biblical teaching, preaching and pastoral care. She shares her life with her husband, the Rev. Thomas Faulkner, their son Christopher, and their energetic rescue dog, Quique.

Alan Jones is dean emeritus of Grace Cathedral, San Francisco. He is also an honorary canon of the Cathedral of our Lady of Chartres and the author of several books on Christian spirituality.

James B. Magness is the bishop suffragan for the Armed Forces and Federal Ministries of The Episcopal Church. Since his election in 2010, he has been caring for Episcopal priests who serve in the Department of Defense, the Department of Veterans Affairs, and in the (Federal) Bureau of Prisons. When not traveling to be with chaplains and members of their families, he maintains an office on the grounds of Washington National Cathedral in Washington, DC.

Daniel P. Matthews is rector emeritus of Trinity Church Wall Street. Having grown up in a small paper mill town in North Carolina, he spent most of his ministry in large downtown parishes. During seventeen years in Lower Manhattan, he was privileged to be a part of international ministry throughout the world supported by Trinity Wall Street. Since retiring, he has been serving the Cathedral Church of St. John the Divine as trustee, co-chair of development, and chair of nominating.

June Osborne is the dean of Salisbury, where she has responsibility for Salisbury Cathedral and is the senior priest of the Salisbury Diocese. She has also served in inner-city and city-center parishes and spends her leisure time watching soccer, reading novels, and pursuing friendships. She is married to a lawyer and has two children.

Brian N. Prior serves as bishop of the Episcopal Church in Minnesota. Before becoming bishop, he served as a parish priest, executive director of a camp and conference center, and vice president and chaplain of the House of Deputies.

William L. Sachs is director for the Center for Interfaith Reconciliation at St. Stephen's Church, Richmond, Virginia. He is also an author, teacher, and consultant.

Edward L. Salmon Jr. serves as dean and president of Nashotah House Theological Seminary and is a former bishop of the Diocese of South Carolina. He spent many years in ministry serving a variety of parishes including in Arkansas, Missouri, and Maryland. He is chairman of the board for *The Anglican Digest*.

Jay Sidebotham is director of RenewalWorks, a new ministry of Forward Movement, and associate rector at St. James' Parish, Wilmington, NC. Jay has served in parishes in Illinois, New York, Washington, Rhode Island, and North Carolina. He draws cartoons a lot, grateful for the material provided by life in the church.

Jennifer Strawbridge is research lecturer, chaplain, and fellow at Keble College, Oxford. She trained for ordination at Yale and Berkeley Divinity Schools and served parishes in Connecticut and Virginia before taking up her current post at Oxford.

Phyllis Tickle, a lector and lay eucharistic minister in The Episcopal Church, is an authority on religion in North America and is the author of many books on the subject. She makes her home on a small farm in rural West Tennessee.

Christopher Wells is executive director and editor of the Living Church Foundation, publisher of *The Living Church* magazine. He studied at St. Olaf College, Yale Divinity School, and the University of Notre Dame, and wrote a dissertation on the Christology of Thomas Aquinas. He lives in Milwaukee where he roots for the Fighting Irish when he is not reading or watching PBS.

Jane Williams is assistant dean at St. Mellitus College, the Church of England's newest theological college, training people for ordained and lay ministries. Jane is a lay theologian and writer whose latest book is *Faces of Christ*.

Mary Kate Wold is the CEO and president of the Church Pension Fund, the organization that provides pensions and other employee benefits to the clergy and lay employees of The Episcopal Church. She is a longtime Episcopalian and has served on the vestries of St. Bartholomew's Church in New York City and Christ Church in Hudson, New York. Originally from North Dakota, Mary Kate has spent most of her adult life working and raising her three children in New York City.

Chris Yaw is the rector of St. David's Episcopal Church in Southfield, Michigan. He is the founder of ChurchNext, which produces and publishes online classes on religion and spirituality.

Marek P. Zabriskie is rector of St. Thomas' Episcopal Church in Fort Washington, Pennsylvania. He is also the founder of The Bible Challenge and director of the Center for Biblical Studies, which shares and promotes The Bible Challenge throughout the Anglican Communion and around the world. He has served churches in Tennessee and Virginia and written and edited several books.

About Forward Movement

Forward Movement has been committed to reinvigorating the Church for more than seventy-five years. While we produce great resources like this book, Forward Movement is not a publishing company. We are a ministry. Our mission is to support you in your spiritual journey, to make stronger disciples and followers of Jesus Christ.

Publishing books, daily reflections, studies for small groups, and online resources is an important way that we live out this ministry. More than a half million people read our daily devotions through *Forward Day by Day*, which is also available in Spanish (*Adelante Día a Día*) and Braille, online and as an app for your smart phones or tablets. It is mailed to more than fifty countries, and we donate nearly 30,000 copies each quarter to prisons, hospitals, and nursing homes. We actively seek partners across the Church and look for ways to provide tools that inspire and challenge.

A ministry of The Episcopal Church, Forward Movement is a nonprofit company completely funded by sales of resources and gifts from generous donors. To learn more about Forward Movement and our resources, please visit us at www.forwardmovement.org or www.AdelanteEnElCamino.org.

We are delighted to be doing this work and invite your prayers and support.